Ben is a trainee accountant working for his family company on the Wirral, Merseyside. He has a wife and a young child and likes to spend his time reading and spending time with his family. This is Ben's debut book.

Dedication

For my family who helped me become
the person I am today.

For Sian, who, without her, I wouldn't be here today.

And finally, Erin:

"No one in this World can love
a girl more than her father."

Ben Thexton

AN UNEXPECTED JOURNEY

Surviving a Brain Injury

AUSTIN MACAULEY PUBLISHERS™

LONDON · CAMBRIDGE · NEW YORK · SHARJAH

A CIP catalogue record for this title is available from the British Library.

ISBN 9781786939043 (Paperback)
ISBN 9781786939050 (E-Book)

www.austinmacauley.com

First Published (2018)
Austin Macauley Publishers Ltd.
25 Canada Square
Canary Wharf
London
E14 5LQ

Acknowledgements

Writing this book has been one of the most challenging, yet rewarding experiences of my life.

I am grateful to my wife, Sian, for giving me the time to write the book, as well as filling in the many gaps in my memory I have had along the way!

Thank you to my family for being there for me every step of the way.

I finally want to thank the NHS, and in particular, the Walton Centre in Liverpool who saved my life thanks to the life-saving care they gave me. You don't realise how much you really rely on the NHS until you need it.

Chapters

1- Introduction

In early June 2012 at the age of 24, my life was turned upside down after a road traffic accident left me fighting for my life in an induced coma. I was a young and ambitious person, with everything to look forward to, when, within the space of a few seconds, it had changed my life forever.

I had gone from planning for my future with my then girlfriend, to coming to terms with a severe brain injury, with the physical, and mental side effects that this brought. One minute I was enjoying my weekend off, and the next, I was waking up in a hospital bed not knowing what had happened to me.

I have mulled over writing this book for a few years. I was uncomfortable writing about myself and my experiences as I felt it a bit self-indulgent. To be honest, I didn't even know where to start. I couldn't articulate how it felt or what I have taken from it all. I found writing it down hard enough, but for years I didn't tell anybody about how I was feeling and what I was going through. But after sitting down and putting my thoughts and experiences in writing, I have felt it quite cathartic, being able to express exactly what it was like. This isn't a self-help book, far from it, and there isn't a magic formula on how to be happy or how to live your life, because everyone is different and have different ways of dealing with things. I am doing this for people who have suffered like me and have not felt able to talk about it or seek help.

Although my book is about my brain injury and what I went through, I want to be able to reach out to people from all walks of life. How I dealt with what happened to me and the coping mechanisms I adopted, I think they can be placed in any situation in your own lives.

Through my subsequent recovery and the sometimes forgotten mental health side effects, I have gone through more highs and lows in the subsequent years than I think most people experience in a lifetime. Being a young man at the time and even after four years at the age of 28, I still consider myself a relatively young adult; most people's journeys through this age period is to "find themselves", whether this is by going travelling, buying a house, getting married, having children, finding a job they like and discovering what it is that makes them tick. I have attempted to do all these things, like everybody else, whilst dealing with the after-effects of a traumatic brain injury. I had told myself since day one of my recovery that I will not let this define my life and I would carry on regardless. Whilst I suppose this is a good way to deal with a traumatic event, it is also extremely dangerous and ill thought. By learning the hard way, I have learnt that effects such as the one that happened to me and, as you'll read later in the book, to my brother, you realise that these events do define who you are and that it's up to you how to use them to your advantage.

Although I did continue to live my life, I didn't come to terms with what had happened for almost four years. I just learnt to manage what was going on, without arousing suspicion with anyone. I couldn't appreciate that something had changed inside of me, the way I thought, the way I reacted to things, and the new thought processes which I had now developed, which were completely alien to me.

Once the dust had settled and the event became today's chip paper, I just continued on with life, not accepting anything had changed. Back then, if someone would have said to me, "you are suffering from anxiety," or, "you are having some type of post-traumatic stress," I would have laughed at them. For one I didn't understand the symptoms, but two, I managed to carry on living my life, so I wasn't "suffering" from anything.

As you will read later in the book, I eventually had to come to terms with what had happened. What was going on inside my head wouldn't go away and it just got stronger and stronger. It was starting to affect my life, both in work, but also in my personal life as well. Life's little "reminders" that you aren't looking after yourself kept rearing their head, and I couldn't ignore them anymore.

Thankfully, I am now in a place where I can sit back and look at what has happened, and understand it better. I can now appreciate what was going on, I can accept it, and, with some self-taught approaches, can deal with them and lead a much happier life, one which I hope will use what has happened to me and my family, to inspire me in later life.

Where I used to look back and be bitter about what had happened, kicking myself over and over again, I can now use it to my advantage. What me and later on, my brother have gone through, are one in a million, and all you can do is accept it, and try and use it to your advantage.

I was left to fend for myself after leaving hospital. Although I had unbelievable support during my time in hospital and subsequent outpatient care for my physical injuries, I was left to deal with the psychological side effects of having a traumatic brain injury and rely on the help from loved ones to assist in my recuperation who, through their own admission, weren't experts in dealing with it. I had changed forever, my whole personality had changed, and, although on the outside I had no obvious effects of my injury, inside I had changed and I had to live with these changes as well as my family.

The main message that I want people to take reading from my story is how I wasted so much time in getting to grips with what was going on. I danced around it for so long, hoping it would go away. Looking back now, it seems so obvious what I needed to do, but when you are in that situation, you can't see the light at the end of the tunnel. If you are true to yourself, then you will work things out and hopefully become happier as a result.

I hope that, after reading my story, you realise how short and precious life is. I nearly lost my own life, as well as almost losing a brother. It took these two blows to my life to realise this and I understand now what life is all about. Worrying yourself about what will happen in the future, something which you have no control over whatsoever, will only end in tears. I have learnt to live more for today as you cannot predict what is going to happen. I had dreams and aspirations right before my accident, I had planned out exactly what I wanted to do with my life, until it was shattered in front of my eyes in the space of a few minutes.

Imagine if you had the opportunity to speak to a younger version of yourself. If you could only tell them one thing, what would it be? I know what I would say. I would tell them not to worry. Things don't turn out as bad as they seemed at the time.

Just something as simple as this helped me so much in getting to where I wanted to be in my life.

I don't want my book to be seen as self-help in any way, far from it. It isn't a doctrine on what you should do or how you should be. It's just my story, and what happened, and how I dealt with things. Even for me to think about it, I can't believe some of the things that have happened to myself and my family, but they have happened and we have come out the other end as better people, and I want to share that with all of you.

If you can take something from it, then that's great. I was a flawed character, and still am even now. I did so many things wrong which I regret. I don't want people to make the same mistakes I did. If you can take anything away from reading my story, then don't regret anything. If you do things which you know are true to yourself, then you won't regret them.

If it wasn't for my family, in particular my wife Sian, and my mum and dad, then I wouldn't be here now, simple as that. They supported me through some of the darkest moments in my life, and provided me with unconditional support and love through these times. They accepted me for who I was, loved me even though I had become a different person and picked me up every time I fell. I was so lucky to have that support network and I want to dedicate this book to them, as without them, I wouldn't be writing it.

Now that I have come off the roller coaster, which has been my life for the past three and a half years, I can now share this journey with you and I hope that you can take something from it.

2- My Life

Born on 26th December, 1987, I am the eldest of three, having a younger sister Amy, and the youngest, my brother Tom. My mum and dad met at a young age and were married at twenty whilst my mum was pregnant with me. Luckily for me, I have supportive parents, who pushed me to achieve the best I could at everything I did, even if I didn't appreciate it at the time!

As the eldest of three, I always had a sense of responsibility and self-consciousness which had come from this. Even though I was usually the instigator of most of the windings up and trouble, I always knew that I had to be responsible when it mattered. Even at a young age and moving into my teen years, I have always been quite anxious, but very driven. This had served me well, ensuring that I performed well in school and developed a good friendship network.

I was a joker, making people laugh and wanting to be centre of attention. I always had been this way and still am now. Again, from a young age and moving into my early to late teens, this helped me socially, having lots of friends and getting on well with people. People always look to you to brighten the mood, whether that is by cracking jokes or doing pranks, and I was always pleased to accommodate!

So, if my early life was on a graph, it would be on an upward curve, achieving the required targets along the way and having an extremely happy upbringing in the process. I was really well supported by my parents to study, do my homework, be polite, honest and follow my goals. After finishing school in

2006, I started at the University of Liverpool on a three year degree course in business and economics.

I met Sian on New Year's Eve 2007 after I went with friends and I met her there. We almost didn't meet that night. I got a ticket at the last minute to go, and, after speaking with Sian for about ten minutes in the pub, she announced that she supported Manchester United! Being a big Liverpool fan this was hard to stomach! I did eventually go back and speak to her though, and we got together soon after. I often laugh with her on how different our life would have been if we hadn't met that night. Speaking on behalf of Sian, it would be perhaps a lot less eventful and stressful!

We often laugh at the first time I met her parents at their house. I wore a Liverpool shirt, as I knew her Dad was also a Man United fan. Not the best introduction but I think we are on speaking terms now!

In 2009 I graduated from the University of Liverpool with a degree in Business Studies. Like many people post-graduation, you aren't sure what to do exactly with your degree. It had been drilled into me from an early age to get the highest education possible and I got to a point where there was a fork in the road, what do I do next? I had achieved all the goals set out in front of me from an early age, but I didn't know exactly what I wanted to do.

All I could be sure of were my hobbies. I loved history. I read a lot of non-fiction, as well as fiction history books and was obsessed with anything to do with local and ancient history. But I wouldn't say I was good at it, in that I didn't have a qualification in history. What I was good at was business, and in particular, numbers. Even with the degree in business under my belt, I did actually apply for a job in the local archive centre. The salary wasn't great, but I thought I would give it a shot. I didn't get the job.

I don't know where the thought came from, but one day I just woke up and thought about becoming a teacher. After toying with the idea for a while I thought that I would be quite good at it and it would be a good career move for me. I thought that, "I'm good with numbers, good at business and economics, why not teach these subjects?" I sold myself on the idea and contacted my old teacher and asked for an opportunity to do some voluntary work at the school, which he accepted. I enjoyed my time doing the voluntary work, I would work with students on a one-to-one basis and also in groups. I sometimes taught some lessons and did after school stuff for students preparing for their exams. It was to give me experience before 0I applied for the post-graduate qualification in teaching.

Up to this point in my life, I did have some sad moments which had left their mark on me. My grandad died in 2003 at a young age from leukaemia which was a difficult time. He was in his mid-fifties when he died so it came as a shock to all our family.

The next major event in my life caught me completely off guard, as they always tend to do. One morning during my time doing voluntary work at the high school, I learnt that one of my best friends from school, Mia, fell ill one night and was admitted to hospital. I had found out that she had collapsed in her bathroom in the evening and once she was admitted to hospital, they found that she had a blood clot on the brain which caused her to have a stroke. She was placed into a coma in the hospital and, once they finally woke her, they discovered that she had no movement from the neck down.

Unfortunately for my friend of only 21, she had locked-in syndrome, which is a condition which causes entire body paralysis, whilst your brain remains completely conscious.

It was a very traumatic time in my life, being so young and for this to happen to my good friend. It made me question life. She was a fit and healthy young person and this just happened out the blue. Why is life so cruel?

Mia returned home after a long spell in hospital, with her family home being adapted for her, with the help of some fundraising later that year. With this happening to such a close friend of mine when we were both still so very young, made me think even at this point how precious life was and that things can happen with the click of a finger.

The way Mia dealt with this cruel event gave me, and probably you, the reader, if you met her, inspiration to live life to the full and not to let things stop you. I am very proud of what she has been able to achieve despite her condition and we remain the best of friends today.

As with anything I suppose you have to carry on with your life. Soon as you know it you are back to the same routine again and things which I thought about at the time when Mia was in hospital about how I wanted to live my life, evaporated and were replaced with immediate goals and targets. What had happened had been boxed away and put in a shelf at the back of my mind and, before you know it, it's forgotten about. I continued on with my voluntary work at the local school and shortly after that, I was admitted onto the post-graduate qualification in teaching.

My relationship with Sian at this time was going well. She had got herself a job in Oswestry as a radiographer, so she had set onto her career path and was doing well. We were both living with parents at the time, so all our spare income we received either went on saving, or on holidays. I've not really been a holiday person, unless it involved doing something history related! But Sian loved them, and she convinced me every time to go on holiday to places I would never think of. We had been to Cuba, Thailand and Mexico within the space of a couple of years. I did manage to sneak in a few things for me, though. We spent weekends away in Bath, Edinburgh and York, where I felt more at home.

I started my teaching qualification in September 2010. I was relatively fresh from coming out of doing a degree so I was no stranger to the academic requirements of completing the course. I had done almost a year's voluntary work at a local school so I was half prepared for life in a school.

I did enjoy teaching, I really did, but there came a point around two thirds of the way through my qualification that I just did not enjoy the bureaucracy of the education system and the rigid approach of teaching lessons. I went into it thinking I would have full control and it would be fun for the kids to learn different things and using a variety of different technologies to portray this. Whilst you can do that, it felt very prescriptive. Plus I was only 23 at the time and I looked younger than most of the students that I taught. Constantly being mistaken for one of them did take its toll and I started to think that I was perhaps too young to enter into this industry.

Whilst pondering over a job offer in North Wales, I was offered a position with the family company. My dad wanted to improve the double glazing side of the business to make it more profitable. Thinking about this now and going back to what I mentioned earlier, whilst I don't love business, I am good at it and thought this could work. I was teaching students how to run a business and make money, I was pretty sure that I could put the theory into practice. I was given an opportunity to have carte blanche over a complete division of a company where I would rise or fall on my decisions. It did excite me thinking about having such a responsible role at an early age.

I can confess that I have never had a passion for double glazing. All I can think about when I think of this is the SafeStyle UK adverts and door to door salesmen. But at the same time, I did like the thought of making money, and it was a new challenge. So, after spending a year training to become a teacher and becoming qualified, I decided to change path completely and started to work for my dad.

Working in a new industry was challenging, but I enjoyed it. The construction industry is very male dominated and it took me a while to become integrated into their ways of thinking. I had gone from university studies, to working in schools, to working in an office and spending time on site. It was a complete change of scenery. I thrived during my early days there, I was one of the youngest employees in the office and like to think that I brought a freshness to the place with new ideas and suggestions. I got the feeling that the more I offered my help, people would look at me and think, "he's quite good at that," and then I would slowly but surely, end up taking this on as part of my job. Being impressionable at the time, I was more than happy to oblige.

Working for a family company, my conscientious side of my personality acted as both an advantage but also a hindrance as I would try and work harder than everyone else, and trying to complete every task to perfection. I was trying to build a business up to make more money for the company, and my family. I would find myself often stressed, but it was manageable as it was the only thing I had to worry about at the time.

During this time, me and Sian started looking for a house. Although she will disagree, I found the house we eventually bought! I spotted it for sale with not a well-known estate agent, and the house looked like it needed a lot of work. The housing market wasn't great at the time, so the price was relatively cheap.

We spent about five months doing the place up between December and May, with the help from both our parents and siblings. As countless readers will appreciate, moving in is one of the most stressful things you can do in your life, and this was no different, working countless nights and weekends to get the house ready. I obviously had no say in any of the interior design elements of the house, I was a bystander to it all. I had "no taste" apparently!

We moved in to our new house at the end of May 2012. The house wasn't completely finished, but enough for us to be able to live there. The move in date fitted nicely, coincided with the FA Cup football final in which my team, Liverpool, played Chelsea.

Life was never better. I was in a new career, thriving on the challenge of making money and working in a completely new industry, and Sian had recently moved jobs to a local hospital which reduced her travel time dramatically.

I had pestered and pestered for a dog but was told, "we have just spent five months renovating our house and you want a slobber machine to come and destroy the place!" To be fair to Sian, the dog I wanted was a French Mastiff, if you don't know what they look like then have a look online and you will get where she was coming from! One of my favourite films was

Turner and Hooch, which has a French Mastiff in the film and I had fallen in love with them since then.

I bided my time before I would ask again.

We had booked a last minute holiday to the Balearic Islands in Spain for a week, we needed the break after working so hard on the house.

Sitting down that weekend, in our new home, both happy and content with where we were in our lives and what we had achieved. I look back now and see myself, daydreaming about where my life was going and what I was hoping for in the future. I laugh now at how in control of the future I thought I was. I had it all sussed out in my head. I knew what life was all about. I was sat there, dreaming away about my future, blissfully unaware of what my life really had in store for me just one week later.

3- The Accident

The 9th June 2012 was like any other day. It was a glorious Saturday morning and Sian had left mid-morning and went to a garden centre with her Mum and Nan, and I stayed at home. I made myself some breakfast, I read the newspaper and watched some TV.

I had to go to the office in the morning as I needed to sort some things out ready for Monday. Our house was only 5–10 minutes away so I nipped out to go and sort things. I knew that Euro 2012 was starting in the next couple of days, so, on my way back from the office, I stopped off at a bookmakers to place a bet on some of the games.

I am sitting here now, scratching my head to see if there is anything else I can remember, but that's about it. Sian has filled in the blanks since then for me. I still have no clue what I bet on either.

I had tried to call Sian a short while before my accident, but she was out at the garden centre. She tried to call me back a few times and I didn't answer. She called my brother, Tom, to see if I was with him, but I wasn't. Finally, on her final attempt of calling, a man answered the phone.

He introduced himself as a policeman and explained that I had been in a traffic accident and I had been taken to the hospital. Sian, probably through nerves, mixed with my practical joke history, asked the policeman if this was a wind-up. "No love, I wouldn't joke about something as serious as this." As I was a joker, Sian thought this was some sick, elaborate prank.

It was at this point that she phoned my parents. They were out shopping and she called them, frantically telling them what had happened. My mum and dad rushed to the hospital, calling my brother and sister on the way. They told my mum and dad that I was in "Resus". My dad told me after that he thought I was being resuscitated. I would have thought the same thing, but Resus is a term used for the A&E department where emergency patients are situated.

Whilst my family sat in the waiting room in the A&E department, they weren't sure exactly what was wrong with me or what had happened. All they knew was that I had been in a road traffic accident, and they weren't allowed in to see me.

They told me that no sooner had they got to the hospital and into the waiting room, they were met by a female Police Liaison Officer. She had come into the family room and called for immediate family only. At this time, nobody had been in to speak to my family, this was the first person. She had briefly explained what had happened, and that they needed to wait for the medical team to come and speak with them. When she left, she left a handful of brain injury charity leaflets.

I dread to think what was going through their heads at this time. Only recently they had been out enjoying their Saturday, and they were now in a waiting room being given leaflets on brain damage. Bearing in mind, this was before anybody from the hospital had been in to speak to them about what had happened. My family didn't even know that I had a head injury at this point.

Sian worked at this hospital, and she knew many of the staff. She says that after the police officer left, she ran over to the CT scanning rooms to see if I was in there. If I did have a head injury, then I would need a CT scan. As she approached the room, one of her colleagues came out. Sian asked if she could go in and see me. They told her no, it's not a good idea for her to see me the way I was. I think that's when Sian started to panic, because if her work colleagues wouldn't let her in to see me, then it must be really bad.

24

Eventually, some of the doctors and nurses came to the waiting room and asked for immediate family. Mum and Dad were next of kin, so were able to go in. But they invited Sian in as well, and they went and sat in a private room to hear what they had to say. Mum and Dad were comforting each other and Sian was sat on the other seat. One of the nurses came and sat by her and held her hand whilst the doctors spoke to them all.

They said that I had been hit by a car whilst crossing the road. The force of the impact with the car had smashed the driver's windscreen, and I had been tossed to the other side of the road, almost being run over a second time by a passing taxi.

Immediately after I was ran over, I stood up and was irate at the driver. Fortunately, a passing ambulance stopped and managed to calm me down and get me into the ambulance, where they restrained me.

I was taken to the local hospital and then assessed by the A&E trauma team. Upon arrival, I was very aggressive and irate, something which can be a good indication of a brain injury. They assessed my head injury immediately by conducting a Glasgow score, which is a test to measure your responsiveness to different stimuli. I scored 3, which is the lowest score you can get, indicating that I'd had a very severe brain injury and that I was entering into a coma.

After they established the severity of my brain injury, they took the decision to induce a coma. So rather than me going into one myself, inducing a coma just means that the medical team take over and put you to sleep. It allowed them to take control of the situation.

They confirmed that I had dislocated my shoulder, I had deep cuts all over my face and chest and had a bruised lung. The CT scan confirmed that I had suffered a subarachnoid haemorrhage resulting in a bleed on the brain and they had also discovered that I had broken the mandible part of my jaw. Unbeknown to them at the time, I had also crushed my left ear canal.

I have quite a large family so as news filtered out what had happened, many of them descended on A&E, one of my family members actually got the train from Yorkshire to come to the hospital. Later in the day, it was decided that I was to go to The Walton Centre, which is a specialist hospital dealing with brain injuries. Sian said that as I was being moved into the ambulance, all my family had lined the corridors as I was being wheeled out.

Upon arrival at The Walton Centre, my family went and sat in a family room, adjacent to the intensive care unit. They were met by a neurosurgeon, an anaesthetist and a senior nurse as they explained to them what they were going to do.

They couldn't say for definite what was going to happen as all brain injuries are completely unique. They couldn't tell them if I was going to make it and, if I did, whether I would have any brain damage after. One thing which sticks in Sian's mind is when she asked them if I did have brain damage, what it would be. They repeated again that every brain is different, but, given the location of the bleed on my brain, the frontal lobe just behind my forehead, that I might have problems with my cognition and speech, and I might not be able to walk again.

At this time, the physical injuries which I had sustained as a result where secondary, as, at the time, this wasn't the clear and present danger.

That first night, my family stayed on the floor in the family room, whilst Sian slept next to my bed. She was sat in the room, whilst the medical team worked on me during the night, keeping me stable and comfortable.

The first step in my treatment was to drill a small hole in my head to insert a probe that would monitor the ICP (Intracranial Pressure) in my brain. Any additional pressures in my brain would make an already bruised brain swell even more and, with the obstruction caused by your skull, can cause secondary brain damage. So, being heavily sedated, reduces the activity in your brain and allows it to heal.

The neurosurgeon explained to my family that they would try and wake me as soon as possible, to ascertain if there is in fact any brain damage to you so they can tailor their treatment to suit. For example, if they tried to wake me and found that I had no movement in my left side or my speech or cognition was impaired in any way, then they could be aware of this as part of my treatment whilst being induced. As well as this, an induced coma is not natural or healthy for your body and, given my age, they were worried I might fight being kept under.

They attempted to try and wake me on the Sunday, fully prepared for me to come out fighting, which is a common reaction when people wake up after being in a coma. I did just that and for a short while they tried to calm me down so they could assess me. It became apparent that I was unable to breathe unaided and they were worried that if they kept me awake any longer, then I might succumb to secondary brain damage if oxygen was being prevented from getting to my brain.

They immediately put me back to sleep and they would try and keep me stable and give me time to heal.

My family waited for news every minute of the day, waiting for updates on what they were going to do next. The medical team looking after me explained that they just wanted to try and keep me stable for a longer period before they did anything else.

Unfortunately, I developed an infection during the course of the week. This caused my temperature to spike to 40 degrees at one point, so they decided to cover me with cooling mats which regulated my body temperature.

The cycle continued for the remainder of the week. I would have a good day, then have a bad day. I would go from being stable, to unstable. It was all a waiting game whilst they tried to give my brain and my body time to heal itself, aware that every day I was in a coma, the more dangerous it would become for me as the chances increased of my body fighting it.

Asking Sian what it was like, to be sat in the family room, not knowing what was going to happen next, she says it was like a roller coaster, you get highs, then immediate lows. You cling on to any piece of good news and convince yourself that I was going to be OK. Then something would happen and it would dampen your mood almost instantly.

They slept on the floor for the entire time I was in hospital. If they were lucky, they managed to put two chairs together to lie on. They spent the night like this, then started a new day all over, checking on me, speaking with the medical staff, and then speaking with visitors when they came. I could not begin to imagine what it must have been like for them, going through all that.

Whilst I was under, my friend Mia came to visit me. Sian took Mia into my room and by my bedside, holding our hands together. Both of them were sobbing and crying, Sian said even the nurse who waited outside was crying!

The thing which got to my family the most, was not knowing really what would happen. Although any time in hospital visiting a loved one is worrying, they explained that you could at least, in most cases, look back at a previous example. In other words, there is a precedent to follow. They could try and piece it all together in their heads. But a brain injury is one of those things that doesn't happen all that often and, after speaking with the doctors and nurses that cared for me, they found it difficult not knowing exactly what was going to happen. As they were told numerous times from the medical team, brain injuries are all unique, and that not one brain injury follows the same pattern. So to some extent, everybody was in the dark as to what would happen to me.

While my family waited in the family room less than 40 yards from my bed, I was in my own little dreamland, totally oblivious to what was going on in the real world.

4- Waking Up

In the eight days I was in a coma, I was in a constant dreaming state, having strong hallucinations and extremely vivid visions of random events. Little did I know what was unfolding in the real world. It wasn't two weeks for me, it was an indeterminate amount of time spent passing through different dreams.

For people that have been in a coma, an induced coma or have been heavily sedated, which I hope there aren't that many, they will understand exactly what I am talking about, the vivid and often haunting dreams. For those that have been fortunate enough not to be, the part when you are asleep is much like having dreams whilst you are sleeping, perhaps after intaking a large amount of dairy goods before bed! But then multiply this dreaming period by eight full days and you get the gist. Through doing some of my own research, as well as speaking with neurosurgeons once I was awake, the hallucinations that I encountered during my coma, were as a result of both the strong sedatives which kept me asleep, and my brain trying to make sense of what was going on. My subconscious kicked in and did the work for me.

I was having a variety of different dreams, ranging from something you would experience I think whilst on LSD, the popular '60s drug, to dreams which involved me being kept prisoner and unable to break out and very scared. All my dreams had a running theme throughout them, I was extremely weak and unable to fight back. Some of the machines that were keeping me alive I placed in my dreams, there was a type of extension lead at the foot of my bed which I placed in my dreams as some sort of device to administer drugs to me. The drug I was taking in my dreams was fed through this device and into my arm on a drip.

I saw many new faces within my dreams, some of them I saw again when I was awake, but in a different setting. It is very frightening, seeing them again in a different set of circumstances, one of the people in my dreams was, in fact, a doctor, but in my dreams he was a drug dealer praying on my addiction. Another person I met in my dreams was a cruel person who kept me prisoner. He was, in fact, my physio who gave me treatment whilst I was asleep. I cannot begin to explain the terror you are faced with when you see these people again after such vivid dreams.

I thought that our new house had been converted by my dad into a care centre for me. But because of the costs of keeping it running, it also housed other sick people as well. I often had dreams which involved me asking for help and not getting any.

Sometimes, I would dream that I was with my parents, and I was trying to convince them that something bad was going on, but they weren't listening. I was being fed drugs by somebody, but they were convinced I was an addict and I needed help. I was screaming at them to listen to me, but they were already walking out the door and I was being left in this room, being fed drugs on a drip.

I would black out, then wake up in a completely different setting. I remember waking up in a barn, and it was a beautiful summer's day. I was unable to walk, so I was sliding along the floor, trying to get outside. As I made my exit, I turned around and a man was there, giving me a menacing look. He approached me and started to feed me drugs.

I was convinced that I was blacking out because I was on drugs and I couldn't remember what I had done. I would wake up, try and remember what had happened, then try and escape from wherever I was.

One dream in particular stands out. I had blacked out, then found myself awake lying on a chair, and I was in my old house, which we had sold to an Indian family a few years previous. I was sat there, with a blanket over me, whilst the family were eating breakfast around the table. I was looking over at them, confused as to how I ended up there. I then panicked and I didn't want to be seen, I thought I would be arrested. So I tried to slide off the chair and make my exit. As I did, the woman in my dreams saw me, and the whole family, without making a noise, just stopped eating and stared at me. The woman approached me and I was trying to explain who I was to her. Then I blacked out again.

This happened to me over and over again.

The day I was woken up, was like any other dream for me. I had a period of blacking out, and then I found myself in a hospital bed, assuming it was at my house. I looked to my right and there was a guy in a bed in the next room lying there. I looked around the room and there were machines everywhere beeping and alarms sounding. I'm not sure how long I scanned the room for, trying to work out where I was.

Eventually, I saw a nurse in front of me and I said to her, 'I need the toilet, do you have one here I can use?' She said, 'No, there isn't a toilet, you can just go.' Not understanding what she meant, I just went. Little did I know that there was a catheter attached to me!

I then asked where I was. She said, 'You are at The Walton Centre, you've had a bang on the head and you have been here for a couple of weeks.' Even at this point, I could not differentiate between dreaming and being conscious, as I had been in a dreaming state for such a long time, and with this came periods of dreams, then darkness, then periods of dreams and then more darkness. It was very confusing for me and I just did not understand where I was at all. I was convinced that I was not where she said I was, I was somewhere I had created in my head. As I didn't have any concept of time either, all I could think about was that nobody knew where I was.

I said to the nurse, 'I shouldn't be here, I need to be at Arrowe Park.' (My local hospital.) I had never heard of The Walton Centre before, I knew where Walton was, an area of Liverpool, but I immediately thought that nobody would know

I was here. 'Get me a taxi,' I said to the nurse. 'My parents and Sian won't know I am here.' 'They know you are here,' said the nurse, 'they have been waiting every day for you to wake up!'

It was at this point that I remember that my dad came in the room and he explained what happened. He asked me a few strange questions, such as my date of birth and the alarm code for the office, which I found strange, but understand it now. He was then joined by Sian, who sat by my side and spoke to me. I remember my first words to her were, "God, you look rough," but her and my dad's subsequent recollection of the events whilst I was asleep proved to be the reason why! I just assumed this was another dream, where I tried to explain to them what was going on, and they wouldn't listen and I would black out again.

But this time it was different, I felt more real. I didn't black out and I was able to speak and actually be listened to. I don't know how long it was before I could differentiate between dreaming and consciousness, but after a short while, I asked what had happened. My family explained what had happened and why I ended up where I was. When they first told me, I looked at them as if they were mad. I almost wanted to shake them and say, "Do you not remember what you did to my house? The care centre?" I hadn't been hit by a car, they were talking rubbish. I know exactly what happened to me. I had been taking drugs and it made me sick. I wanted to find somebody else from my dreams to verify my story but I couldn't see anybody close by.

The confusion of not knowing exactly what had happened is a really surreal feeling. You aren't sure whether you are dreaming or if you are awake. I was convinced that I had been awake all this time and that everybody was mad, and I was the only sane one in the room. Even when somebody reiterated what happened, I would just pay them lip service, pretending that I agreed with them, but I was inwardly thinking that they were talking rubbish.

I don't know how long this lasted. But slowly but surely, people and things that I remembered in my dreams started coming into vision. I would start questioning myself then, wondering whether I was actually wrong this whole time. I was so confused.

People ask me what went through my head when I was awake. I told them it's not like in a film, where you see people waking from comas, jumping out the bed. You just wake up, as if from a deep sleep, and it takes a while for you to come to terms with what has happened. You cannot think much past your immediate thoughts. You don't really think of anything at the time when you wake up. You are just confused and you are convinced that you are in completely different circumstances to the one you are actually in.

One thing I did notice when I started to become more aware, was how much pain I was in. My whole body felt broken, I felt as if I had been battered.

Once I was more or less awake, I was told by my family that I was being filmed by a production company doing a documentary for a nationwide TV station. They asked if I was happy for them to film me whilst I met the neurosurgeon who would explain what had happened to me. I was too out of it to protest so I accepted, something which I regret doing now, because it was aired about six months after my accident and, although it made people aware of what I went through, it opened up wounds for my family which I regret. I didn't find it intrusive really. To be honest, I wasn't really that bothered that they were filming. I know that my family weren't happy with them filming, but, at the time, I didn't really care that much and thought that it would be good advertising for the hospital.

During my chat with the neurosurgeon, he explained that I had suffered a "closed head injury" resulting in me having to be kept asleep whilst they waited for the swelling to heal. He explained that the risks in doing so are quite high, as your body will naturally fight being sedated, as you are acting for the body, in particular, respiration. With someone as young as myself, this can have disastrous consequences as often your body fights the sedation, meaning that you are more heavily sedated, increasing your recovery time, but also putting you at risk of further brain injury as you are kept asleep for longer. Luckily, my body hadn't reacted too badly and after around ten days they woke me up. Watching my consultation with the neurosurgeon back on the TV show six months later I just cringe at myself. I was completely out of it.

The first thing I wanted to do was to go home. The problem was that I had forgotten how to use my legs. I knew how to walk and stand up but I couldn't get my legs to do it for me. I had lost all strength in my torso to pull myself up. Luckily, as the doctors said at the time, I am young and that I will get my core strength back.

I could not eat properly, being fed on a tube meant that my swallow reflex had gone, so every time I tried to drink something I would cough it up. I was aware that something was wrong with my mouth, unbeknown to me the injury meant the lower part of my jaw was on an angle. When I bit down, the bottom half of my jaw was on one side. At first I thought that I had some sort of facial defect after my accident.

I was still in a lot of pain from bruising so I didn't notice my shoulder in any discomfort. It all just mixed into one, my entire body all feeling the same. I had lost quite a lot of weight. Before the accident I was about thirteen and a half stone so I looked quite thin considering I am six foot one.

Although at the time, I did not lament or reflect on what had happened, to think about it now it is surreal to recollect that just two weeks previous I was settled in my job, happy with my new life with Sian and in our new house and I was now sat in intensive care after nearly dying, with physical injuries which would take a while to heal and mental side effects of the accident which may never recover.

After a day or so of being in the intensive care unit I was slowly waking up and gaining strength back. I was starting to get frustrated being in the bed all day and not being allowed out, if I was, then it was in a wheelchair to the outside courtyard. I remember speaking to Sian outside and she said to me, "Do you remember anything about being asleep?" "No," I said. "Do you remember me saying anything to you?" I couldn't recall anything really, it was all a haze. "I promised that if you woke up, I would get you a dog." "Well," I thought, "at least I get a dog out of all of this." There are much easier ways of getting your own way!

After a day or so, the doctors did their rounds one morning and said that I was ready to be transferred to a general ward. I didn't need to go on a high dependency unit, as, once I was awake, I didn't have any other health problems which required a high dependency level. So I was quite pleased that I had skipped a step in my recovery. That afternoon I was moved onto the Dott Ward, with my brother pushing me in a wheelchair through the hospital.

I didn't enjoy the ward at all. I had a band on my wrist which indicated that I was a fall risk, which meant I couldn't leave the bed. It made it even worse sharing a ward with ten to fifteen other people. I had nothing against them, they were all sick and needed attending too, I just couldn't bear being there. After my first night in the ward, I didn't sleep at all. The drugs I was on made me very sleepy, so I slept a lot in the day so I was awake at night. As the ward has strict visiting hours, I could only see my family for a short while in the afternoon and at night. When I was on intensive care, I could see them whenever I wanted and it was less strict when I could go out and when they could come in. I suppose they restrict visiting times to give you chance to heal, but, after spending so long just lying in bed all day, I craved human interaction.

In the daytime, when I couldn't really do anything other than sit in bed, I would go over to the ward reception and offer to make the nurses cups of tea. I would speak with them for a bit until they told me to go back into my bed. They had TVs and I could listen to music, but I couldn't really enjoy any of those things because I couldn't concentrate on anything for too long.

England were playing that night as well and I remember my friend Nick coming to the hospital that evening and we watched the football in one of the waiting rooms. It was a spectacular fall from grace, I could imagine me and Nick watching the football together in different settings, perhaps in a pub, perhaps in one of our houses, having a few beers and laughing. But I struggled to keep up with the game, it was making me dizzy watching it and trying to pay attention to what was going on.

I woke up the following day, which was a Wednesday morning on the ward, just three nights after waking up from my coma, determined to go home.

What sealed it for me was waking up one morning and asking the nurse if I could go for a shower. She said, 'you can, but in one hour and you can't have a shower without help.' 'What does that mean?' I said. 'Well, you can't walk around on your own so you will need someone to help you shower.' Fair enough, I probably needed help to shower, but I still didn't want to be "assisted". I know that when you are admitted to hospital you leave your dignity on the door on your way in, but it's still tough to take. I was escorted by an elderly nurse to the shower room and stripped off naked, careful to keep my back to her at all times. Despite my injuries and inability to lift my arms properly and sat in a shower seat, that was the quickest shower I have ever had!

So, once I was showered and back in bed, I waited for the doctors to come around to start the process of getting discharged. If you have been in hospital before, you know the doctors come round and talk amongst themselves about you, and I overheard them saying that they would give me until the end of the week because I was due to have an operation on my jaw at a different hospital.

I interrupted them and said, 'I'm leaving today, there is nothing wrong with me and I really want to go home.' The doctor said, 'I don't think it's a good idea, as you might be a seizure risk and you have an operation at the end of the week.' I said to them that I had been doing crosswords and Sudokus for two days and my brain was fine, and if I did have a seizure, then my family were around to help. I know this is a stupid thing to say, but I was desperate to leave the hospital. He said to me that I needed to be discharged from the physiotherapist, occupational health, have my stiches out, and then finally, by the neurosurgeon. So, I knew what I needed to do and set about planning my exit that day.

I managed to see the physio that morning, so my wristband came off and I was free to walk around. I then arranged an appointment to see occupational health, who would carry out an assessment on my brain activity. The tests they did were actually really hard, maybe that's because my brain had been shook around in my head after the accident and was still a little swollen, but I swear they were hard, a bit like an IQ test. What made it worse was that after my initial recording with the TV guys upon waking, and, with my agreeing to them filming me, they had carte blanche to follow my escapades around the hospital to get discharged. I didn't really acknowledge they were there, I just wanted to get out!

By the time the afternoon visiting came around, I had arranged for my neurosurgeon to come to see me and then, hopefully, discharge me at about 4.30 pm. My dad and brother had gone to a county show as I had told them I am fine and they should go as they go every year. Sian was visiting me, as well as my mum, so I had to break the news to them. They weren't happy. They couldn't understand why they were letting me go so soon. But if they hadn't have done, then I would have gone anyway because I couldn't spend another night in hospital. As well as that, I remember thinking that, "I'm not that ill, and the bed I'm in can be used by somebody who needs it." My mum wanted me to spend some time at home, bearing in mind that I had only recently moved out of my parents' just a few weeks before. But I didn't want that either, I wanted to be in my new house, with Sian, and start rebuilding my life again.

The way I saw it, I was out of danger and I felt OK, so why couldn't I go home? Nobody could say to me, this is wrong with you, which reinforced my determination to go home. I suppose if I had woken up with obvious brain damage, then there would have been some additional services which I required, but I passed all of the tests required to be discharged. Even then, I thought to myself, "Well, they didn't know me before the accident, so just because I am passing the tests doesn't really mean I'm OK." But I didn't really care at that point, I couldn't stay in the hospital any longer.

Even now, if I asked somebody at the hospital whether I had any long lasting effects, they still couldn't answer the question. The bleeding on my brain had stopped, the swelling had reduced and I was awake and walking round. Anything else which might have happened, they couldn't tell me for sure. The only people that really could determine that would have been my family. What else can the hospital do?

I had never been through this before, and neither had my family. I wasn't sure what I needed to be doing, or what would happen to me. All I was sure of, were my feelings on wanting to go home. Nobody could give me a good reason to stay in hospital. Sure, I was tired and bruised, but there wasn't anything medically wrong with me. If I had a problem with my brain, then I would have it whether I was in hospital or at home, and there isn't anything that anybody could do for me, as I wasn't given any answers over what I needed to do to make myself better.

I was discharged later that evening after finally speaking with the neurosurgeon. My mum took me home, I think Sian had gone back home to get the house ready for me, as she hadn't spent any time there since my accident. I remember driving back from the hospital, still not fully digesting what had happened to me. I was just fixated on going home.

Pulling into the drive of our new home, it was still an unfamiliar place to me as I had just moved in a week before. But this is where I wanted to be. I was a grown man, had just built a life for myself and I would get through this myself, or so I thought at the time.

I walked into my house that evening, ready to start rebuilding my life again.

5- Coming Home

What do you do after an event such as this? Should you be grateful? Should you feel lucky? Should you feel depressed after what has happened? For me it was euphoria, I was happy to be out of hospital and alive and relatively able. I just didn't have any other thoughts at this time. It felt as though I had been on a roller coaster at a funfair and that feeling you get when you first come off is what it was like. You just don't have the mental capacity, or energy, to think of anything else. I suppose my brain was busy trying to fix itself, leaving no room for a period of reflection. You live day to day as you haven't got any energy to think past what you have got to do right that minute.

The first thing that I needed to have sorted was my jaw. I left the hospital on the Wednesday with it still broken and with me looking like Marlon Brando. My operation was for that Friday, so it was another trip to the hospital, and a period of sedation. I woke up on the Friday afternoon after the operation, to find that my jaw had been wired shut. It is like a brace you would have fitted, although it's much more bulky and it was very sore, as it effectively puts your jaw back into position. I was told that I would have to have this in for about eight weeks, at which point they would assess whether my jaw had healed enough for it to be removed.

When I switched on my phone when I was back at home, I noticed that I had quite a large amount of Facebook notifications. People I had not seen or spoken to for years had given me their well wishes, in particular when I was asleep.

This was a nice thing for me to see, knowing that people cared about me and that they were concerned about my well-being.

The first couple of days and weeks back at home, I didn't think about anything, I didn't have the energy. I was prescribed liquid codeine, which made me out of it for most of the time. I was eating liquids through a straw which, when you consider my substantial weight loss after the accident, was difficult for me to put any weight back on. My girlfriend had taken time off work, so I had company the whole time. My parents visited most days and, when I felt up to it, I went round to theirs.

I had received a ton of leaflets from the hospital, including brain injury charities, counselling and other support groups. But I was not interested in any of those things. I was in too much pain and had other things to deal with. So I threw them in the bin. I wouldn't sit there and read leaflets. Why did I need to speak with a charity about my brain injury? I didn't think I required their services at all. I had been discharged from the hospital and they wouldn't have done that if I wasn't OK.

My days consisted of watching Nothing to Declare Australia, sleeping and eating. I was starting to get bored. After being on the go my whole life, I wanted to do something and get back to normal. A week after being discharged from hospital I asked Sian to take me out somewhere. So her parents took us to Erddig Castle in Wales. We were there for a few hours, but soon after walking around for a short time, I felt extremely faint and wanted to lie down. This set me back for a while, I was bound to the sofa for another week, unable to do anything.

The weather wasn't great at this time, so I was confined to the four walls of my home, not able really to go out and get fresh air. Sian tried to coax me into doing some things round the house to keep me busy like baking. I am not Paul Hollywood and I had no interest in baking at all. I appreciated what she was doing for me, but it annoyed me even more thinking that my life had come to baking cakes and cookies to keep myself busy.

I was a ghost of my former self. I would look at myself in the mirror, much skinnier than I had been only a few weeks earlier, my eyes were glazed over, through being tired and through the drugs I was on. My face still looked battered, with cuts down my right side of my face which had been glued together in hospital. I had scratches all over my chest and it hurt to even move a little bit. I looked at myself, I wasn't sure whether to laugh or cry at how I had ended up. At this time, I wasn't really thinking how I would look in the future, I didn't really care. I was in too much pain to even care at this time, but it felt like a spectacular fall from grace.

I didn't really feel any pain from my brain. I didn't think I had any pain there that was for sure. I almost expected that I would have some sort of pain there, I had been told I had swelling and bruising, so I assumed I would feel this in my head. Where they had drilled into my skull on the right side of my forehead, that was quite sore, but, apart from that, I was just in pain everywhere else in my body. So, my priority was to get rid of the physical pain I had, not anything to do with any damage in my brain.

Most of the eight weeks after the accident were quite blurry, but I certainly remember the day I had out my "arch bars" from my jaw. I met the maxillofacial doctor who gave me two options at the time, I either had anaesthetic in my gums which would take about an hour, or we did it the hard way and just pulled them out. I chose the latter. I still cringe now thinking about it. Effectively, you have a metal brace attached to your teeth which are fixed with metal pipe cleaners into your gums and are screwed in. So for about an hour I had the doctor, with a pair of pliers, unscrewing these metal screws, counting down from three, and then pulling. Even now I wince at the pain, the splatter of blood and the throbbing discomfort after. But my jaw was better and I could now eat properly; still very weak though, so no toffee for me just yet!

I had visited the fracture clinic shortly after my jaw was sorted. They had confirmed that I had actually broken my shoulder, as well as it being dislocated. Bearing in mind this was almost two months after my accident, it just showed me how important everything else was at the time. I was so spaced out on pain relief, that I hardly even noticed any considerable pain there.

I had been given a physiotherapy course, to improve the healing in my shoulder and, shortly after, I got a letter through the post from a nutritionist for an appointment to see if I had put weight on and I was eating OK. I was still struggling to swallow things down. It was almost as if every time I ate or drank something, it made me gag. It did subside after a while, but it was a strange sensation to experience. I had been taking "build up" drinks to help me put weight on, especially when I wasn't able to eat anything solid for the first two months.

Everything seemed to be going OK at this point. I was still getting over what had happened, and had too much to think about with all my physical injuries to worry about anything else at this time.

I remember the Police Liaison Officer coming round to my house one afternoon, to go through what had happened. I vividly remember that I felt as though they showed no real compassion for what had happened. I got the impression from them that they wanted to ensure I didn't take it any further. I didn't even want to. I accepted that the person who knocked me over couldn't have stopped and I felt bad that she had to witness what she did. But most of the interview consisted of them reminding me that it was my fault and if I were to put a claim in then I would lose. I just wanted to forget about what had happened, not that I could remember it anyway. It was way too soon, I thought, for them to be coming round anyway, I didn't feel in the right frame of mind at the time and I wasn't ready to talk about it just yet. But I suppose they have a job to do and the case needed to be closed, so I can understand why they came round. But, once they had left my house, I never heard from them again.

I was getting more and more frustrated as the days turned into weeks after being discharged. I remember having a copy of the day's newspaper in front of me each day, trying to do the crossword and Sudoku puzzles. I could do them, but a lot slower than I would have been able to normally. I was certain that my cognition hadn't changed, I felt just as able as I was before my accident. But something had changed. I just knew I wasn't the same person.

To articulate the feeling, it was like presenting me with a scenario before my accident, and then presenting me with the same scenario after the accident and I would deal with it completely differently. Even at this early stage of my recovery, I knew something had changed. It was almost as if my brain had been re-wired, so I would react to things differently.

Often, if something happened, such as Sian dropping something on the floor or even saying my name, I would get the feeling to scream and shout at her. It was almost an involuntary thing that I couldn't control, and often I couldn't control it. If I was talking to somebody and they didn't understand what I was saying or needed me to repeat it, then this would invoke a similar reaction. It was like something inside me was making me react to things which didn't warrant, or deserve a reaction. But I couldn't help it. But back then, I thought it was everybody else's fault, they were the unreasonable ones for not understanding me or because they were saying my name too many times or dropping things on the floor.

What made it worse was that people would try and understand it and offer remedies to help me such as calming down, breathing, and going to sleep and relaxing, all of which would make me even angrier. One, because they didn't understand at all, and two, because these things were not what I wanted or needed. What they, and even I couldn't understand, was that these reactions and behaviours were things that I couldn't control. To put it into perspective, it's like someone poking you with a pin or sharp object, and you react to this, whether you want to or not as the receptors in your brain react involuntarily to pain. That was what it was like, you could not prevent it from happening. Once it had happened, I knew it was wrong, I knew that it was an unreasonable outburst for something trivial.

That's not to say it happened all the time. I would behave normally for a good period of time, then, usually when I was tired or had done quite a bit during the day, I would reach a threshold where I couldn't cope with stuff anymore. It was like starting the day with your brain energy levels half full, then getting up, getting dressed, having breakfast, speaking with people, watching TV, reading the newspaper and doing the crossword, you are left with hardly anything. So when something happened which would have usually invoked nothing inside of me, I would have an outburst of irritation or aggression against what had happened. The person who usually got the brunt of this was Sian. Usually, she would not react to me behaving like this, she understood what was happening. But, she hasn't had to deal with this before, so how many times could you expect her to put up with it? She was also back in work, which meant she would come home, and sometimes want to vent herself, or her energy levels were also low. Sometimes during my recovery period, I would see her pull into the drive, after a day in the house like a caged animal, almost licking my lips at the prospect of some human interaction, only for it to end up in a massive argument over something trivial.

"You haven't got a clue what this is like," is the response I would give to her if she tried to understand it or offer some guidance. Not only had I suffered in terms of brain energy levels, I also had a different outlook to emotional reactions to things. If Sian wanted to talk about a bad day at work or if something had upset her, I didn't react the same. I wouldn't see it as a big deal and would always revert it back to my own suffering and how bad it was for me. I was selfishly wanting to keep reminding her that what I had suffered was much worse. I was alone and everybody else was acting strange, not understanding things as I did and not having the same reactions to things as I did. If people got upset over things, this would

44

get me confused, or even irritated. Why would you get upset over this, it's nothing?

I was booked in to see a variety of different medical professionals about my physical injuries and my recovery in that respect, but not once did I see a doctor about my head and how I was feeling. It was my fault I suppose and I should have identified that something was going on at the time, but I didn't want to admit it. You can't hide a bad shoulder, or a bruised body, or weight loss, so I had to deal with these and get them sorted out, but I could at least try and hide my internal problems.

I couldn't socialise anymore. I couldn't deal with a social situation where there was more than a couple of people in a confined space. Part of it was thinking people were looking at me to see if there was anything wrong with me, like I was an animal at the zoo, but it was more that I couldn't deal with having a conversation if there were other people talking at the same time. It would get me confused, which turned into irritation. I would want to immediately get out of the situation and go somewhere quiet. I never suffered from any sort of social anxiety, far from it, I always enjoyed being centre of attention. I did try and pretend that I was still the same person and nothing had changed, but this was virtually impossible after a while. If I got to this point, I would make my excuses and leave. None of my friends or people I socialised with, would have any idea what was going on.

Why couldn't I be that person anymore? That's what made me who I was. But now, I couldn't think of anything worse.

Aside from my family and close friends, I felt uneasy with other people. They just didn't know how to react around me or how they should behave around me. I would get annoyed because I felt like saying to them, "I am exactly the same as I have always been!" But I could tell that when they spoke to me they held back, or didn't speak to me properly. I felt as though I was being treated like a baby and I was being patronised. This was the opposite of what I needed, I wanted to be treated normal like everybody else. This reaffirmed my decision to try and keep myself to myself. I didn't want to be put in the situation where I would feel uncomfortable, both for me and who I spoke to. It would have made it a bit easier, I thought, if I wore a badge on my T-shirt, saying that yes, I have been in an accident and my brain is a little damaged, but I am OK and you can treat me normal!

I got the impression that when people looked at me, they were expecting to see something a lot worse. They were almost surprised at how well I look considering. I think that reinforced some type of prejudice, in that I looked OK so I must be OK. It's not their fault, I would have probably done the same given the circumstances. It's a lot for somebody to comprehend. There are few people that would have had to deal with somebody after a brain injury and wouldn't know how to react.

You look for obvious things that you can comment on, such as your physical condition and whether you feel OK in yourself. I don't think anybody ever spoke to me with regards to what was going on inside my head. It was almost as if they were scared to ask, or they didn't think that anything was wrong at all as I seemed so fit and able.

Once I had met somebody for the first time after my accident, and, once they had spoken to me and asked if I was OK, then they resumed their lives as normal, like any normal person would. They had done their "bit". But I was still left with what had happened and I didn't have a clue what to do for the best.

The one word which would sum these feelings up would be frustration. I was frustrated that this had happened to me and nobody else, and I was frustrated that I was angry and feeling irritable all the time. But I didn't think that I had changed that much, I was adamant it wasn't me, it was everybody else.

I was angry and upset that my life had changed forever in the space of a few weeks. Why did this happen to me and why am I being punished? I started to feel self-pity, but also pity for Sian. She had just bought a house with me and she had aspirations of her own, and this had put a halt to everything. At this point in my recovery, I didn't have a clue how I would end up, whether I could function as normal ever again, go back to work and lead a normal life. I was scared about the future. I was trying not to think past the day to day, but I started to envisage what my life was going to be like. I had worked hard all my life to get to a decent position, for it all to be taken away by something stupid. I was regretful in not crossing the road with more care. Why did I not just look properly and none of this would have happened?

It felt as though I had lost my identity. The old me had been knocked out of me in the accident, and it was replaced with a new me which I didn't recognise and neither did my friends or family. It was a confusing time because I did recognise what I was like before my accident, but now I was behaving completely differently and I was feeling ashamed of myself. I didn't like the person I was becoming. I didn't like how I was reacting to things and behaving. It felt like I had been hijacked by a virus, similar to getting having your identity stolen online. They are using your identity, using your bank cards, accessing your Facebook and your emails and pretending to be you. You are trying to tell people this isn't me, but the more and more I was hijacked, the more it stuck. It was so frustrating because I couldn't do anything about it.

Becoming tired was something which happened a lot as well. By about 8 pm each night I would go to bed. I had nothing left to give after then. If I was kept up past that time I would turn into a monster. I coined a phrase, "I'm on my last legs." If I said that, then it was time to go to bed. Sian was really understanding about it all. She knew I needed the sleep.

Speaking to Sian looking back, she knew I had changed, but didn't want to say anything to me at the time. She didn't want to say anything to me out of fear of how I would react, but she didn't want me to worry or feel worse. She told me that before what happened, I would be fun and happy-go-lucky and, within the space of only a couple of months, my whole demeanour had changed. Where once I would laugh at things, instead I would get angry and irate. I think what made it most difficult for Sian was the way in which I showed no emotion. I wouldn't be interested in anything she had to say, I didn't show compassion, empathy or understanding of things she wanted to talk about. Looking back now, Sian suffered just as much as I did, and she was equally reluctant to speak out and get it off her chest. She too felt like she had nobody to talk to.

You would think that after what happened, this would bring us closer together. It did, we have both shared things together that not many couples go through and we had become much closer. If anything, Sian had become my carer, especially in the first couple of weeks of me being back home. She had helped me shower, helped me into bed, made sure I was eating enough and all general day to day things which I needed help with.

I know that Sian was with me in hospital all that time, willing me to get better. Even though I wasn't conscious, I was aware of her presence, and I am sure that, without her, I would be much worse off than I turned out.

What we were both doing was bottling things up in our heads. I wouldn't tell Sian anything and she wouldn't tell anything to me. She wouldn't say anything through fear of how I would react or fearful of whether it would make me take a backwards step. At this point in my recovery, I wasn't overly aware of changes to myself, and I certainly wasn't feeling guilty about them. Anything that was going through my head at this time I kept bottled up. I kept it bottled up to protect Sian and also my family as they had been through enough. So, through protecting each other from any harm, we kept things from each other. This lasted, for me anyway, for well over three years until I couldn't keep it from her anymore, which will appear later in the book. It is crazy to think back now at what we both did, through an act of kindness to each other, we actually made the situation worse by not talking about it.

I felt upset and angry that me and Sian had found each other, fell in love with each other's personalities and decided to spend our lives together. In one moment, this had all changed, I had changed. Sian had fallen in love with the "old me" and had happily decided to spend her life with me. I had changed as a person and she would have to deal with that if she wanted to spend her life with me. I thought at the time that she might not want to do that. She had come into this expecting one thing and ended up with another through no fault of her own. I was beating myself up over it as I knew that the real me was inside wanting to come out, but I couldn't.

What frustrated me the most was that I had it in my head that I had been discharged from hospital, so I must be OK. I didn't think for one second that I would change. It didn't even enter into my head that my personality would change, that I wouldn't be the same person. Even during this time, I was adamant that this was just part of the healing process and that it would pass with time. I don't think there was one time during the early days, where anybody said to me, "Ben, you've changed." They all just thought it was something which happened and then went away. I certainly wasn't conscious of my behaviour or actions. I can only see it now after a longer period of time.

As time went by, "the accident" and the side effects of it became the elephant in the room. We all knew it was there, but it wasn't really spoken about. It was brought up in a jovial way, but nothing ever serious. Nobody could fathom what to do for the best.

After the first couple of months after the accident, I felt as though it was in the forefront of everyone's minds, it was still so raw for people. But, as time passed and I started to improve, people got on with their lives as normal. I felt as though I had now been left with what I had been left with, and perhaps I needed to try and get back to normal as well.

6- Road to Recovery

I was slowly starting to come to terms with dealing with the changes to my brain and how I dealt with things. I just adapted myself to living with them and developed coping mechanisms. My brain hadn't changed as far as me being able to do things on a cognitive level. But I was getting very bored, I hated being at home, just sat there doing nothing all day. I had nothing to keep my brain occupied. Family and friends were all imploring me to rest and relax, but the more I did, the more bored I got and the more my mind wandered. I have never been the type of person to sit and watch TV all day, or sit still for that matter. I have always been on the go, always had something on which required for me to be on the go.

When I was first out of hospital, I had no choice, because my brain wasn't in the right state of mind to allow me to think this way. I found it impossible to concentrate on anything for very long. But now it did and I needed to do something about it. Plus, nobody could actually tell me what was wrong. Yes, I had physical injuries which were still healing, but my job wasn't physical so that was irrelevant I thought. As I said before, I didn't feel any different, and I felt more than capable of fulfilling my daily tasks in work with no problem, so I didn't see any big issue with me returning to work.

I was definitely in denial. All my behaviours at this point steer towards it. Although I knew something had changed, I was completely pig-headed about it all. I did, at some points in my recovery, get a bit down in the dumps, thinking that there was no way back from this. That it had happened and the damage would be here forever. But that was counterproductive I thought. So, thinking this way, helped me to bottle things up even more and deny what had happened over and over again. Eventually, I thought, it would sort itself out.

At the age of 24 and before my accident, I remember thinking that I had my immediate future sussed out and I knew where I wanted to go, but all that had changed. In the greater plan of life, I didn't know what I wanted to do and who I wanted to be.

I didn't know what the world was all about at that age and still don't know even now. So for me to try and make sense of what had happened to me, as well as living my life in a way I wasn't yet sure of, was impossible. I wasn't long enough in the tooth to appreciate life. All I knew was studying for most of my life, living with my parents, getting a job and moving into a new house, then this. All I could do at this point was to try and get back to normal, and I figured that the only way I could do this would be to do exactly what I was doing before my accident.

At the end of July, I started to go back to work part- time, taking calls and answering emails. Bearing in mind I had been running a division of the business for the family company, I was starting to stress about how it was being run and whether things were going wrong. If I was working for another employer, then I am sure that I would not think like this, but I am conscientious, as well as taking the job personally as it had such close ties with my family. I was also being paid whilst being off and I felt guilty that I was being paid for doing nothing.

Boredom wasn't the only thing which drove me to work. I had developed an approval trait in my personality. I was young and strong and I was wanting to prove to everybody that the accident had had no effect on me whatsoever and enjoyed any praise I got which indicated that I didn't look any different or didn't act any different. I thought at the time that this positive feedback on my recovery speeded things up and helped me get better. I only know now that this positive reinforcement made me bottle things up more and more and the thought of admitting that I wasn't fine and that I was struggling, would somehow make people think less of me and set me back.

I wanted to prove it to myself as well. I wasn't going to let this change anything, I still wanted to carry on with my life as normal, and this was just a small setback. I had never had to deal with a brain injury before so I just assumed that it was like any other injury you would have and if the hospital were concerned about me at all, then they wouldn't have let me go. Nobody could convince me otherwise and I was able to make my own decisions about my life and I would deal with it my way. I was aware of changes to the way I behaved, but I thought these would be temporary, and the coping mechanisms of positive reinforcement from people, as well as carrying on with a normal life, would combat these changes until they ceased to exist.

I wouldn't say that I had a road map to recovery, it was more I wanted to forget about it and get on with life as normal. I was back in work and I was trying, where possible, to just get on with it. So fresh after the accident, I was only aware of a few subtle changes, which I could suppress to outsiders, and act as if nothing had changed. If I did have a wobble, then I had a "free pass", people would be understanding and think that I was still getting over what had happened.

I was young, it had hit me like a ton of bricks and I wasn't sure how I should react. I just thought the best thing to do would be to carry on with life as normal. I didn't really have much responsibility other than our new house so I had no real precedent to follow on my road to recovery, I just thought, "I'll go back to work and see how much I can do."

At this point in my recovery, I simply didn't think about anything to do with the intricacies of my brain injury and the implications it had on my life. I wasn't aware of anything tangible that I could treat and I certainly didn't want to admit or confront whatever it was, I just dealt with it my way and hoped for the best.

I planned to visit the hospital one weekend with my family to give the intensive care unit and the Dott Ward some cards, chocolates and flowers. Going back, I didn't really feel anything really, I didn't really remember much from being there, I could have been at any hospital and I wouldn't have recognised anything. I spent 99% of my time asleep or in a bed so I didn't really get to see what the hospital looked like and where everything was.

We went to the intensive care unit first. Going in for the first time, I recognised only two things, the smell and the noise. The beeping of the machines in particular sent shivers down my spine when I went in. I must have heard them going off constantly whilst I was asleep and it did bring it all back to me then.

Quite a few nurses came over to me and asked if I was OK and how I was doing. I was being greeted as an old friend and as if I should know who these people were, when I didn't recognise them at all. They told me that they had all treated me during my stay, but apart from one nurse which I remembered from my dreams, I didn't remember any of them.

We also visited the Dott Ward briefly and I saw nurses from my brief stay there. They commented that I was a pain in the backside when I was there. I was certainly a pain when I was here, because all I wanted to do was go home.

The bruising in my body was still very sore, but after a few months this had subsided. It was at this point that I noticed that I had no hearing in my left ear. After initial consultations with the GP, he decided to send me to a specialist who, after conducting a scan on me, discovered that as a result of the impact of landing on the floor, it had pushed my jaw bone up and crushed my ear canal.

I would need an operation to drill a new ear canal into my left ear. Great! But at least I would hopefully have my hearing back. For anyone that has partial, or full deafness in one ear, you will understand that having deafness in one side can make your balance go, as well as struggling to hear conversations with background noise, so you are reluctant to enter into conversations with people as you are conscious of this all the time.

After a period of being in work, I started to struggle. I could not deal with the simplest of tasks. Even writing an email or arranging materials and labour for a job, would give me a headache and I could not concentrate properly. I was often tired and would leave work early anyway to rest. I was adamant that I did not want to go back home and do nothing. My parents and Sian sat me down and said that I had returned to work too early and that I needed more time off. I pleaded with them to let me stay in work, I knew that if I went home the boredom would set in and the darkness would return to my thoughts.

They wouldn't have it. So I was sent back home to rest again. I knew it was the best thing for me, but I just didn't know how to deal with the boredom that I would inevitably encounter. Being only 24 at this time, I didn't really have any hobbies, other than playing sports such as football. I was also an avid reader, but I couldn't read a book for longer than half an hour.

I had the problem of my brain capacity stopping me from doing anything arduous for long periods, coupled with having physical injuries to my head and body which prevented me from doing any sort of physical activities. I had also been banned from driving until I was discharged from the neurosurgeon, which was still a few months away. I did not know how I was going to cope.

Part of me knew that I was tired and that I needed to leave early because I was tired. One day, I told someone that I wanted to leave because I was tired and they rolled their eyes. It felt like to me that they were thinking, "You're either in work, or not at all." But I couldn't do either, I wanted something in the middle, that's what I thought I needed.

After this happened, I just tried to avoid telling people I was tired. People think you are lazy, I thought, or perhaps you are going to bed late and not getting enough sleep. It's not a good enough reason to go home early. But it wasn't just tiredness, I thought to myself. It was brain tiredness. I couldn't give any more to the tasks I was doing during the day. I couldn't think straight and I was getting confused. That made me tired, and that's why I needed to go home. But I couldn't articulate that properly at the time and it made me bottle it up as a result.

This was a crushing blow to me. The coping mechanisms which I was so confident of working, had failed me. I had to admit defeat to everybody I knew and was sent packing, back to home, and back to another period of sitting there and doing nothing. What went through my head was that nobody was understanding what was going on. This was the opposite of what I wanted. How would I get better if I could not stretch myself to get my brain back working again? If I was to sit at home all day, then surely it would get worse and not better? I felt as if they wanted to stick me at home as an out of sight, out of mind tactic. They thought that this was the best for me, to leave me at home to get better, forgetting completely the person I was before the accident, assuming that they were dealing with a completely different person, when, in fact, I was the same person, just a little damaged on the inside.

What was annoying me was that I wanted to be treated normal, but at the same time, I got the impression from people that, now that I was out of the woods and OK, that I must be OK and didn't need any support. I didn't want to be stuck at home, being told to rest and recover. I wanted to try and get on with life as normal.

What frustrated me more than anything was how black and white it was treated. I was either better or I was sick, there was nothing in between. Why couldn't I just get on with life normally to a point, then come home and relax when I needed to? But there didn't seem to be a compromise, I was either back in work full time, or I was off sick completely, shut off from the world.

After my physical injuries had all subsided, it just left me with these "hidden" injuries which nobody knew about. It wasn't their fault that they couldn't see them. You can only see what's in front of you. As well as that, I felt that if I did tell people what was going on, they wouldn't know what to do and it would make it awkward.

Things that were happening on a daily basis, such as me snapping at people, becoming tired easily, feeling overwhelmed and confused, I wasn't sure whether this was because of the accident, or just normal for people who work full time. I couldn't tell for sure. On the one hand, I would have people treat everything I did as a result of my brain injury. Then on the other, I had people saying that what I was experiencing was just because I was working hard and doing lots of things. But how would I know what the difference was? I was in denial, so I took to option two. This was just what people went through when they work hard. Sometimes I felt like screaming, "I can't help it!"

If somebody could sit down and tell me what behavioural traits that could have changed, then perhaps I would have been more aware of them. If I behaved a certain way, I would immediately feel remorseful and sad that I had behaved like that. I became frustrated because that's not how I wanted to be as a person. But my head was spinning round and round, trying to work out whether this was "old me" or "new me" Was I always like this? If so, I needed to stop it and refrain from behaving like this. Or was this the new me? In which case, there isn't anything I can do. But I couldn't tell the difference, not at this point anyway. "Your injury is at the front part of your brain which is what makes you who you are." Thanks for the advice, but can you tell me whether the entire part of this brain is damaged, or just a portion of it? If so, what portion is damaged and what this means for me? Silence. I looked at brain like this. If I was brain damaged then I would be less intelligent, but, I didn't feel any less intelligent so I can't be brain damaged.

What I didn't appreciate at the time was how my brain was processing the information. Even though my intelligence hadn't suffered, how I was reacting to the outside world and the information it supplied me, had.

But, I knew they were right. I could feel that I wasn't right, I just didn't want to admit it to myself. I knew already, without anybody telling me, that I was doing too much. I could feel my body tire after only a few hours of doing something. I would just ignore it and fight through, but I wasn't kidding anybody. I was seriously fatigued, without realising it. After a few hours of being in work I would become "foggy", I couldn't really understand what people were saying to me and I couldn't concentrate on what I was doing. But I just tried to get through it and hope that it goes away. I just assumed my brain needed a "dusting down" after being out for so long. But it didn't need to be dusted down, it needed to heal. It is like any other muscle inside your body, it needs time to heal, and not be over stretched or over used. That's what I was doing to it and it didn't like it.

I have had muscle injuries before, and I wouldn't dream of trying to play sport if I had torn my hamstring, but it's OK for me to try and make my brain work through an injury. How do you deal with letting your brain heal? I was young and driven, I didn't want to be sat at home letting my brain heal. I did feel OK for periods during the day, where I would start questioning whether there was actually anything wrong with my brain. I just didn't know what to do for the best. The people around me didn't know either. There isn't one set of answers for everybody, as injuries to your brain are all unique, the brain is so complex. So how would anybody know which part of the brain was wanting to heal? I just felt tired and foggy after a period of time, that's all I knew. But you don't tell anybody, otherwise you sound like you're complaining all the time. I was a grown man, I couldn't imagine saying to Sian or my parents, "I don't know what it is, I just can't do things, I can't concentrate and I feel tired." It's not an accurate diagnosis, it's not something that people can identify with and don't know what the best solution is for you. So the best thing they offer you is for you to stay at home.

After a while of being sat at home, I started to over think things. I was getting myself into a frenzied state of panic and anxiety. I had never dealt with these types of feelings before, so I couldn't identify them at the time. Being sat at home all day, when all you want to do is to do something useful, my mind wandered, to the point where I was in quite a bad way. I would over think things to the nth degree until I started to worry about people, in particular, to the scenarios I had thought up in my head and if they ever happened. For example, I would call Sian when she was in work, if she didn't answer after a couple of times, then I would panic. Why isn't she answering her phone? Has something happened? What was the last thing I said to her? Was I rude to her? I can't believe that I never told her I loved her when she left for work because she annoyed me this morning. I would sometimes think about what was going on in work with me not being there. My job role had been separated out and given to different people to manage. Even though I was off work, I still had my smart phone so I could access my email account, so I would see what was going on. I would see an email and think, "oh my God, what is going on here". I would firstly start to worry about it, then it would get worse, then I would try and action whatever it was. But I was off work so I was told to keep out of the way and it would be dealt with. But nobody could deal with it better than me so it was going to be done wrong!

It was like an itch that you have on your back. You try and ignore it, then you have to scratch it, but the itch doesn't go away, it just stays there. That's what it felt like to me. I was on an endless cycle of panic and anxiety during my second spell of being at home and it was so tiring, waking up every day, knowing that it was coming. I wouldn't tell Sian what was going on, or my family. I still had enough reserves to pretend like nothing had happened. I suppose they knew that I wasn't myself all the time, but they wouldn't suspect anything else.

There were times during dark periods whilst I was off work where I would feel like telling somebody, but I always stopped myself. Aside from not wanting to admit it to anyone, I also felt guilty in burdening people with even more problems, after everything that they had been through with me just a few months ago. I was adamant that I would keep it from them and shield them from any more worries about me. I would sort this out myself in my own way.

I obviously knew that there were people that I could speak to, there was a brain charity called Headway which we had a leaflet for I think just after the accident and was handed to my family. But I wasn't the type of person that would sit in a room with other brain injury survivors and open up all my scars. I just wanted somebody to explain to me what I could be faced with going forward, a more accurate prognosis. The problem is, that there isn't one. Doctors can guess what might happen, but the brain heals in different ways, and everybody's brains are completely unique. I just had to be aware of any changes to my behaviour, movement and cognition. I had to develop stronger coping mechanisms to tackle the turmoil inside my head and hope that it goes away eventually.

It was like a double edged sword. I was dealing with the side effects of the brain injury, which were related to my emotional reactions to situations and how I had changed as a person. Not only that, I was now dealing with the alien feeling of feeling down, of feeling panicky and having strong levels of anxiety as a result.

The trouble I was having ceased for a period when, one Saturday morning I was outside in the garden, seemingly the only sunny day that summer. Sian had said that she was going out with her mum to do some shopping. I was sat in the sun reading the newspaper. I remember falling asleep on the chair for what must have been a few hours, when I could hear someone calling my name, and it sounded like they were crying. 'Who's that?' I said. Then the back gate opened, and Sian was stood there, holding what she promised me in hospital, a dog!

It was the dog I always wanted, a French Mastiff. Not great if you have a nice new house, with all their slobbering, as Sian liked to remind me, but I didn't care. We named her Dotty, after the time I spent on the Dott Ward in the hospital. She had got the dog slightly earlier than planned, in light of me being sent home from work. She thought this would keep me occupied whilst I was off, and she did.

Dotty needed and wanted my attention most of the day. Dogs, and domesticated animals in general, will give affection, with no strings attached. They will treat you and view you the same. They don't ask questions about how you are, they don't question you when you react to things and everything they offer you is unconditional. It was exactly what I needed. Dotty was with me for those few months where I was at my lowest, always by my side and never asking for anything more than for me just to be with her. We formed a special bond, even though she didn't realise it, Dotty has seen and heard as much of the bad side effects I suffered during my recovery and never once treated me any differently or tried to understand it. It might sound stupid, but, in her own way, she saved me from getting any worse.

I met the neurosurgeon about three months after being discharged from the hospital. At this point, I was feeling physically, a lot better. I again returned to the hospital. It's not really the building that sends shivers down your spine, or the fact of what happened to me here, all I ever thought about was the smell. As soon as you go in, the smells came back to me straight away. Not only that, but I noticed that it was still a busy place. I naively thought in my head that they saved my life and that they deserved a break after such a traumatic time. But you forget that once I have gone, there are other sick people waiting at the door for life saving treatment. There is no rest for them and it made me appreciate how amazing the hospital was.

When I met the neurosurgeon, I sat down, opposite him. He didn't look up, he was reading my notes. He eventually looked up and said to me, 'You've had a bit of an ordeal, haven't you?' I said, 'Yes, just a bit!' He spoke to me at length, exactly what happened to me during my stay in the hospital. I was quite surprised that they didn't speak to me about the accident, he was only interested in what they had found on the initial scans and what happened to me once I was in the intensive care ward.

He said that my recovery, considering my early Glasgow score of three, was remarkable. He was happy to say that I could drive again as I was no longer a seizure risk. I also started playing football again, in an attempt to get my fitness back. I did ask him, whilst I was there, about the change in my mood, the slight change in my personality, and my emotional reactions to things. He went on to explain to me that a lot of brain injuries happen at the frontal lobe, the part behind your forehead. Within this frontal lobe, contains everything which makes you who you are. Any damage to this can cause you to change your personality, as well as your mood and tolerance to things. That would explain the changes in my personality which I, as well as family and friends, had noticed. I asked him what this would mean for me moving into the future, to which he explained that subtle changes to who you are cannot be shown on a brain scan, these are changes which have happened as a result of the brain injury and can only be noticed by yourself or people around you. He said things such as my mood, my personality, my emotions, as well as my planning and preparation skills, can be affected. I didn't know it at the time, but it was there and then when I really should have accepted what had happened and learned to live with it. That was the point where I should have asked for help.

7- Keeping Busy

Although things were going in the right direction, and with Dotty keeping me occupied at home, I was still having frequent, and prolonged periods of feeling low and anxious. Even with Dotty there by my side when I was off work, they found a way of getting back into my mind and causing damage. The more I tried to understand what it was, the more I started thinking to myself that perhaps these were just normal thoughts. In my head, I thought to myself that everybody must experience the same sort of thing. Being young at the time, and prior to the accident not really having any responsibilities at all as we had only recently moved into our new house, I just assumed what I was feeling was the everyday stresses that people have when they have responsibilities like a new house and a job. Added to that I was still recovering from my accident, I thought it would pass. I knew that I was bored, had nothing to do, and, as a result, my mind wandered. I was in a bad place, and nobody knew.

I was a great actor, my family were oblivious to the whole thing, they may have noticed some changes in my behaviour, but they didn't know what was going on inside my head at that time. They might not like that I kept it from them, but at the time, I didn't want to admit it myself so I certainly wasn't going to talk to somebody else about it. In addition, it eased after a period, so I knew it would pass. I was just itching to get back to work and keep busy. It wasn't so much that I wanted to get back to work, it was more that I had some comfort in work, knowing that my brain was being kept active all day, not affording me any time to sit and ponder things endlessly all day. There was a strange comfort in knowing that, if my brain was occupied doing something else, it wouldn't find any time to torment me. This then planted the seed for the next period in my life.

I returned to work shortly after my consultation with the neurosurgeon with my new idea of trying to "keep busy" to offset any of the side effects I had. One of the main causes of my panic and anxiety, was what people thought of me. This was both in what they thought of me after my accident, and also what they thought of me as a person and how good I was at my job. My way of getting rid of one of these feelings, was to make sure that I "pleased" everybody, making sure people had a good opinion of me. This was mainly a work thing. Now that I think about it, being off for a few months had made me think that people were starting to think I might be "milking" it, and that there was nothing much wrong with me. That made me try and keep everyone happy, whether that was through working as hard as possible, or by helping people in work do their jobs as well. Whatever it was and whatever the cost, I would make sure that, whenever anybody ever thought about me, the first thing they thought was, "he's a hard worker."

To combat the anxiety of dealing with the future and trying to control it, I would make sure I kept busy and kept things in the pipeline to look towards during times of feeling low. Alongside keeping busy all the time, I would always try and keep things in the back of my mind that I could start immediately, in the event of me feeling anxious.

To combat me thinking about the brain injury and how it had affected me, I would just adopt a self-pity approach. I would think to myself that what I have been through is not what many people would encounter so if I feel bad about it then so what. The problem you have, as many people with similar symptoms to mine will understand, is that all this is invisible, it will only come out if you are becoming irate or you are openly quiet or low. If you had broken your leg or had any other physical injury, then people would see it before you even spoke to them. The problem with things that go on in your head is that the only way of making people understand is through talking to people and telling them. Even if I had, not many people know how to deal with it, especially people that have never dealt with it before, and will offer their solutions to try and get you better. It never got that far, I wouldn't tell them.

To combat feeling tired all the time, I would go to bed as early as possible when I came home to get as much sleep as I could ready for the next day. I was also finding that eating in the morning or at dinner time, would make me sleepy. I could manage snacks no problem. But anything more than that would make me want to fall asleep. I'm sure plenty of people feel like having a nap after a large lunch, but this was after just a sandwich and a packet of crisps for me. So, to avoid this happening, I would not eat as much during the day, which would keep me awake and alert. I made up for it at night by eating my evening meal, then supper. I didn't have any weight loss, if anything, I put a bit on, probably because I was eating at the wrong times and the wrong quantities. But I was able to manage in work and living my life if I followed this rule.

To combat the personality and emotional changes to myself, then I wouldn't combat them at all. The way I thought about that at the time was, well it's happened, and this is what I, and my family, have been left with and it is what it is. That part of me cannot be changed. I was pretty sure that my family would rather me be alive, in a slightly altered way to what I was, to me being not here. I just denied it was there at all. I just accepted that they were "quirks" and that they were here to stay. One thing that I struggled with was when I behaved in a certain way or did something reckless, then I couldn't differentiate between me behaving that way because it was "me", or behaving that way as a result of what's happened.

What helped during my second spell back in work was that my physical injuries were starting to heal up, I felt OK although I still had one thing which I still had in the pipeline. My ear operation was due in November 2012 which I wasn't really looking forward to as it involved drilling a new ear canal into my ear!

When I returned to work, my job role had changed. Our company secretary, who ran the accounts department within the business, was going off on maternity leave, meaning that I was to now run this department, as well as keeping a glancing eye over the windows department which had been given to somebody else to run for the time being. At the time, I was happy with this. I was a little sad that I had to focus my attention on accounts, something which, again, I'm not passionate about, but I'm good at. It also provided me with a new and fresh challenge on my return back to work. We had employed another member of staff to help as well which I thought would make the job a bit easier. I was actually quite proud of myself, that I was trusted to run the accounts department of a decent sized business, given that I wasn't 100% back to normal. I would repay this faith shown in me.

My new coping mechanisms were in full force as well, working away in the back of my mind. Whenever I felt any symptoms coming on, I would just find something to keep myself busy, giving my brain something else to think about and distract it. I would treat these symptoms as some sort of devil on my shoulder. If they were allowed to speak, they would control my life and drag me back down. But if I kept busy, then they were being overcrowded by other things keeping me busy so they weren't able to cause any damage.

The only thing that I knew would happen every single week, was when I arrived at Friday, and into the weekend. Friday morning I would come to work, and it would slowly start to take over my mind and thoughts, so, by the time I got to Friday afternoon, I was in quite a low and irate mood. This would start a cycle off, which involved me coming home, finding something to argue with Sian about, and then setting a tone for the weekend. If nothing was planned for the Saturday or the Sunday, I already knew that I was in for a rocky ride that weekend. Rather than develop yet more coping mechanisms for the weekend blues as I would call them, I would just hope that something was planned, and would spend my time wishing for Monday to arrive when I would be back in the comfort of my office at work, where I would be kept busy and trouble free.

During my second spell in work, I noticed that I had started to become a bit obsessive over things. This was both at home and also in work. I have never been a neat freak or had any type of OCD, but I was becoming aware of my obsessiveness over things. If I was in work, the second anybody spoke to me, I would write down what they were saying, like I was a policeman conducting an interview. I'm not sure whether this is because I was scared I would forget, but I couldn't sit and listen to somebody talking without writing down what they had to say.

At home, there was a strategy war game that I liked to play. I would play it once every couple of days and I would do the exact same thing over and over again, exactly the same strategy. If something happened different to how I set it out, then I would quit the game and feel frustrated. I would have a list of jobs to do in the office, and there was no way that I could go home without that list being completed in full. I couldn't even contemplate going home, knowing that I had some items on the list still not done.

I treated this new personality trait like I did with all the others. I denied them. I almost convinced myself that I always had them in me, but the bang on my head made them more extreme. If anything, the obsessiveness increased my intelligence, because the more obsessed I became with things, the more I knew and the more intelligent I became. So I almost treated it as a bonus! I was obviously forgetting that if things didn't go to plan, or I couldn't complete whatever task it was to the nth degree, then I would become frustrated.

I would sit in work or at home, thinking about the world in general. I would think about politics, wars, current affairs and local community projects and think about the many thousands of unresolved things there are. I would drive past a development on my way to work and look at it, half finished, and it would drive me mad that they hadn't finished it and it needed completing. Like the anxiety I was suffering, it was like an itch that I couldn't scratch. The only way that I would be able to calm down, would be to do something familiar to appease myself. I would take the dog for a walk, walking the exact same route. I would play the war strategy game, exactly the same way as I always do. Looking at myself now, I didn't even contemplate any of this at the time, I just did them without any thought.

More so during working hours, I would find that I often repeated myself. I didn't do it because I had forgotten what I had just said, I would repeat words or sentences over and over. I went in to see my dad one day and I said to him, 'the accountants are coming in on Tuesday,' 'coming in on Tuesday.' I would do this all the time. It was a source of amusement amongst me and Dad that I would do this. I never thought that this was because of my accident, I just thought it was one of my many quirks!

Me and Sian decided to go on holiday, we both deserved a break. I was a little concerned that I might not get travel insurance for going, but I was adamant that I wanted to go away. So in November, we went on holiday, travelling to Egypt for two weeks. Before we went away and, to be honest, as soon as I was awake in hospital, I had decided that I wanted to propose to Sian. I wanted to do something a bit different, I had an idea to create a video, with me talking to her, then showing images before asking her to marry me at the end. I had contacted a company before I went on holiday and we arranged to meet when I came back. Before we went away, I needed to go to Sian's parents' house to ask her Dad for his permission. I found an excuse to go one afternoon and, after quite a long period of chit chat, I plucked up the courage to ask. He stood up, shook my hand, and said, 'That's fine Ben, you'll be OK, you're pushing at an open door anyway!'

The holiday was great, a pretty typical holiday to Egypt. We saw the Pyramids, we saw the Sphinx, and we visited Cairo and sat in the sun the rest of the time. I had nothing to worry about really, just getting up in the morning, picking a book to read and picking somewhere to sit and sunbathe all day! We tried to book a trip to visit Petra in Jordan and go to Jerusalem, but trouble had started in Israel so this was cancelled. I enjoyed going away on holiday and sitting by the pool, but liked to keep some days aside for exploring.

To look at us both sat there in the sun, you wouldn't even look twice, we both looked completely normal and at peace, despite everything that had happened. Sian banned me from taking my phone with me, to stop me talking to people about work. She took her phone, so, during the holiday, I just wanted to "check in" with my dad to see how it was at home. Really, I was talking to him about work. Not the best thing to be doing when you are on holiday. But even then, I wanted to at least keep my brain ticking over and thinking about things. A couple of times during our holiday, I did get a little anxious, thinking about back home and that I was far away and unable to do anything. So calling back and checking in calmed me down.

My ear operation came shortly after the holiday, and I had a short time off work whilst I got over it. It wasn't as bad as I thought it was going to be, but I had an attractive lump of cotton wool in my ear for a month or two with some sort of bandage covered in a disinfectant which was pushed inside my ear to keep the newly drilled hole open. It's as nasty and smelly as it sounds!

When we came back from our holiday, I met up with the video producer company. I had picked a song I wanted to be played in the background, which was a song by Mumford and Sons, called Lover of the Light. I actually heard the song on the radio on my way to meet them, and instantly decided to use that song. I spoke with Sian's sister, Helen, about going and picking the ring. I didn't have a clue what ring to get her and how much I should spend. I had heard from someone that you should spend three months' salary on the ring. But, if you know me, you would know that I can be quite frugal! Me and Helen picked the ring one day after work and she took it home to keep safe until the big day.

Christmas morning 2012, I took Dotty on her usual walk, I was walking with her, nervously preparing myself to pop the question. I had it all planned in my head and how I was going to do it. I repeated the plan over and over in my head. I had the ring in my pocket, careful not to drop it on the field.

I played her the DVD, she had no idea whatsoever. At the end of the DVD, I said, 'I have one more present to give you.' It was funny seeing her face, when she realised that wasn't the end. I did the normal thing, got down on one knee and asked her to marry me. She said yes!

We entered a new year and the documentary which I was filmed for was due to be aired. It was being shown on a UK TV channel. We were watching TV one night when an advert for it came on. Me and Sian both looked at each other and butterflies went through my stomach. I felt like I was doing so well to get over what had happened, and was worried that this would bring some of it back. At the time I was happy to do it, it didn't really bother me. But now I regretted it. I was mainly worried that people would start to talk to me about it again, asking more and more details.

When I watched the documentary, it was quite hard to stomach. I basically watched the nurses and doctors, first hand, trying to save my life, while I was lying there, lifeless. It showed them bringing me round, then not being able to respond or breathe properly. It showed the neurosurgeon talking about me and what they planned on doing next. It then showed the interview I did with the film team, and it was quite embarrassing as I was talking quite a lot of rubbish, but I said to Sian at the time, 'that will be the drugs making me say that!' One things sticks in my mind though.

'Are you hungry?' asked the neurosurgeon. I said, 'Well, the food isn't exactly top standard, but I am hungry, yeh.' This guy had literally saved my life and all I could do was moan about the food! It was crazy to see me, looking so vulnerable, battered and bruised, speaking into a film camera. You would think that if you did ever make it onto TV, it would be in more glamorous circumstances!

After the show finished, I received quite a lot of messages from people. Before the documentary went out I was worried about what people would message me, but once they did, I was quite pleased, and surprised, that most people commented on how well I've done to come this far and that they didn't realise at the time how serious it was. At least it gave people some perspective on the situation and it gave me a little boost knowing that people thought I was doing so well, thus far.

I was tired quite a lot of the time, especially towards the end of the week. I have always woken up early, around 5 am, and then got to work early. But I didn't have a good balance, I would get to work early and finish late. I would combat this by just going to bed early, around 8 pm or 9 pm each night. Sian did get frustrated with me that I was going to bed so early, but, my reasoning with her was that if I stayed up any later, then I would become irate and grumpy. "You need to spend more time with me and less time in work." I agreed with her completely, but I needed to be in work, or at least kept busy most of the day so I could function properly.

A year or so passed and me and Sian carried on life as normal, me working full time in my new role and she working full time as well. We finished most of the work on the house as well and we decided on a wedding venue, which was in Frascati, near Rome, in May, 2014. My brother was going to be my best man and my sister was Sian's bridesmaid, along with Helen, her sister. All the while, any sniff of my symptoms creeping into my head, were shut back away with my effective coping mechanisms.

The 26th May, 2014, was the day of our marriage. It was a beautiful sunny day in Italy and, in honour of tradition, I spent it away from Sian! I spent the day with my friends, sat in their room and by the pool, reminiscing about what we used to get up to when we were younger. I wasn't really nervous about getting married or delivering a speech. I was more nervous that I had brought so many people to a foreign country for our wedding and I wanted everything to go to plan.

Getting married was the best day of my life, being stood up in front of friends and families, in the evening sunshine, looking out at Rome in the distance. I thanked everyone for coming and for all the support they had given me over the years since my accident. Who would have thought that just two and a half years earlier, I was lying in a hospital bed, with my life hanging in the balance and now, I was able to marry my wife and spend it with my family and friends. The turmoil I had faced in the months after my accident and the internal battles I had faced, seemed a very long way away at this point, as I drank, sang and danced the whole night away with my new wife and all my family and friends.

We had arranged to go on honeymoon the day after we returned to the UK. We had booked a round trip to Las Vegas, San Francisco, Hawaii and Los Angeles. The trip of a lifetime to cap off the wedding of a lifetime.

Once the dust had settled after such an eventful occasion, it was back to normal for both of us, and back to work. It was around this time that, after an external audit of our company from a big accountancy practice, I got chatting to our auditor, who told me about how he ended up where he was. I had thought about making my new role within the company more official, by getting a qualification in accounts. I already had my degree, but I wanted something more specific. After taking some advice from the auditor, I decided to apply to do the chartered accountancy qualification. This was a hard course to take, especially when working full time, but I was determined to do it. I would study during the evenings and take the exams during exam periods throughout the year.

In September 2014, me and my family did a charity fundraiser for The Walton Centre, the hospital that saved my life. It was a charity zip wire off the top of the Port of Liverpool building in the city centre. The event was to raise money for the "Home From Home", which was something they wanted to build for families to stay overnight whilst their loved ones received care. During my stay in the hospital, my family often spent nights on the floor in the family room and we all thought this was a great cause to raise money for. I also wanted to give something back after they saved my life.

It was around this time that I was contacted by a local newspaper. My dad had recently been interviewed about the business and how well it was doing in the north-west area. He had mentioned me in the article and I think they saw what happened to me when it made the papers and put two and two together. I was happy to do the article, more so to give the business a bit of free advertising. It was also quite nice for me to think I was being recognised for how well I was doing. I did cringe a little when I saw the article and the headline they used!

As I entered a new chapter in my life, now happily married and my new life to look forward to, everything which had happened, as far as I was concerned, had been boxed away and forgotten about. I had managed to achieve everything I wanted to do in my life, not letting what happened affect me too much.

I thought I had won, I had beaten the odds that were stacked against me and come out the other end victorious. I had managed to live my life, dealing with the brain injury and what it did to me, by using my coping mechanisms. Yes, I was busy all the time and working harder than I needed to, but if that was the price to pay for me to have a normal life then so be it.

I was loving life again, excited for my future together with Sian.

8-   Sian's Got News

Our early married life was great. We had experienced living with each other for over a year, so we knew each other's little quirks and managed through the teething problems of managing a house together, no problem. It wasn't exactly a normal start to living in a new home, so if we could manage that, then we could manage anything else that came our way.

I was working hard on my accountancy course, working evenings and weekends to prepare for my exams. I was determined to have a recognised qualification for the current job I was doing, and I wanted this extra feather in my cap.

My life would change forever once again one night in December, 2014 when I returned home from playing football. My wife was sat on the sofa and said, "I've bought you something." It was something inside a Tesco's bag. When I opened it, it was a Babygro with Daddy on it.

She was pregnant.

This topped getting married. What a feeling this was. I was so happy. As my wife works as a radiographer for the NHS, she needed to inform her employers immediately once she knew she was pregnant, so she didn't really want to tell her employers before her family, so that night, we went round to both parents and told them the good news.

My mantra of "keeping busy" was working well. Anytime I felt any hint of feeling low or anxious, I would just put something in the way of it. I had more than enough to keep me occupied for the foreseeable future and the feelings I could feel stirring would be suppressed every time. The weekend blues would be welcomed like an old friend, and pass as Monday morning arrived and I came to work and forgot about it. I used to think that the anxiety was like a virus, and it needed to attach itself to something. So if I could feed it with a tangible, anxious situation, then I would be happy being anxious of that, rather than concocting things inside my head.

I did feel fatigued often, but this wasn't a problem. I would come home from work and fall asleep soon after. Sian was pregnant and tired herself so it was a win-win situation for both of us. During the evenings and at the weekends, we didn't have much on most of the time, so I had the necessary time to recover and rest.

Christmas 2014 fast approached and Sian started to get morning sickness as I am sure many people do when they are pregnant. As Christmas Day and Boxing Day came and went, Sian wasn't eating or drinking. She was bed bound for about three days, unable to keep anything down, until one day I decided that I needed to take her to hospital because I was worried she wasn't able to stay fed and hydrated and was worried it was putting the baby at risk.

We arrived at the hospital in the maternity section and they admitted her straight away. I was quite worried at this time as I had no idea what was wrong with her. I thought morning sickness was just something women got when they were pregnant and it passed during the course of the pregnancy. When she was admitted they wanted to conduct a series of tests. They wanted to do a scan of the baby, they wanted to rule out ectopic pregnancy. I didn't even know what ectopic pregnancy meant but it scared me.

In the end, they said she had acute morning sickness, the same thing which Princess Kate had with her first child, or so I'm told. She was in hospital for about three days and discharged just before the New Year. Although these types of things, you would think, would make somebody very anxious and worried, they did for me, but I have suffered from anxiety and worry at a heightened level since my accident. If anything, stuff like this I thrive off, because I don't feel guilty for having these feelings, I had a legitimate reason to feel that way. That seems quite strange for even me to say it, but when something like this happens to me, it's like a welcome relief, because I can then feed the anxiety for a bit longer and it remains attached to the circumstances.

After this event passed, we both carried on with our lives and got back into a routine of working and looking after the house. I felt quite accomplished, more so that I had tackled what was going on with self-taught remedies which were working. I felt like I had an endless supply of things I could attach my anxiety to. Work was very accommodating in that respect. With the change in my job role into accounts, this provided me with a daily dose of events which would feed my anxiety. Working for a family company was stressful, full stop. But throw into the mix the constant fight for money, chasing people for payments, then not being able to pay people, with them ringing my personal mobile over and over again, although it did annoy me and stress me out, it did offer me an escape route, so if someone said, "Ben, you look anxious," I could say, "yes that's because this person keeps phoning me."

We had been spending time doing the back garden anyway before Sian fell pregnant, but with this happening, it sped things up. We had used the money from our wedding to have the work done and it was almost complete, barring having the patio laid and painting the fences. I also got the front garden done as well during this time, so everything was complete.

We had a nursery to decorate and furnish as well. What was once my home office now became the baby's new room. All my furniture from this room was relegated into the dog's outhouse!

I was thriving on the endless supply of things to keep me occupied, quietly satisfied with how I was coping. This all changed for me, as it always does, on the day of Sian's 12 week scan at the hospital. We went in the afternoon for the scan and everything was OK, the baby was doing great and doing everything it should be doing at this stage. We both returned to work and agreed to let everyone else know that night who we hadn't already told.

I went to play five-a-side football which I always do one evening a week. During the game, I was hit in the head with the football. At the time, I didn't even react, I didn't stumble over or feel groggy at all. I returned home from playing and went to get me and Sian some pizza. Sian was trying to take a picture of the scan photo next to Dotty to use when she announced to everyone she was pregnant. I was laughing as I left the house at how uncooperative Dotty was being!

On my way home from collecting the pizza I just started feeling funny. All of a sudden, I felt like I couldn't breathe and I went very cold, but sweating at the same time. What the hell was happening? I had to pull over in the car and give myself some time to calm down. I had no idea what it was but it really scared me. It was like I was being possessed by something. I couldn't control my body or my breathing.

After about five minutes sat in the car I composed myself enough to drive home. When I got in I went straight upstairs and splashed cold water on my face and sat on the toilet seat for ten minutes to try and appear normal.

I looked at myself in the mirror, my eyes seemed glazed and I felt groggy. I needed to pull it together. Sian was about to announce to everyone she was pregnant, this was supposed to be a good day, don't ruin it by having a funny turn.

I didn't know what had happened to me. I tried to convince myself that I had been a little light-headed after playing football and not having anything to eat. But I was just kidding myself.

I went downstairs, smiling as I walked down as Sian continued to fight with Dotty to get her to keep still. I helped her take the picture, she told her friends and we ate pizza. Episode over and I had gotten away with not having to tell her.

The morning after, I went to work as normal. I felt OK and I carried on with my daily tasks as I had done the previous day. A few people I spoke with that morning asked if I was OK. "Yes, why?" I said. "You're not making sense." "Are you sure?" What were they going on about?

I was sat at my desk and my dad came into my office and said, 'I'm taking you to the hospital.' 'Why?' I said. 'You're not right today, something isn't right with you.'

Driving to the hospital, I asked him what he thought was wrong, because I didn't feel any different. 'You have been talking to people this morning and not making sense. You've been repeating yourself and getting confused.'

I still didn't believe him and thought taking me to the hospital was a bit of an overreaction. When I got there, Sian was in work so she was sat with me, along with my dad and my mum who met us there.

I had a variety of tests done on me whilst waiting for a doctor to see me. When he came to speak to me, I tried to remember everything that I had done the previous day. I remember forgetting my date of birth, having to look at the wristband on my arm to verify the date. I couldn't even remember my date of birth? What was going on?

I soon remembered that I played football that night and explained that I had been hit in the head with the football. But I said it wasn't that hard and I barely noticed it. They immediately said that I had concussion and that was the cause of the symptoms I had been experiencing.

Fair enough, I thought. If that's what they think. I was discharged soon after and told to take a few days off work to recover. I still don't think to this day that I had concussion. I thought that the force of the ball hitting my head wasn't enough to cause concussion. I was convinced that something else was going on.

For the remainder of Sian's pregnancy, I probably worked as hard as I had ever done. I worked long hours, keeping myself busy in work. At night, I would come home and study for my accountancy exams. I became obsessed with having at least four exams completed before the baby arrived and was determined to get them completed. I did manage to do them and passed all four.

We were busy in the house at the weekend, getting everything ready for the arrival. If I felt tired of a night or of a weekend, then I would go to bed as early as possible. Everything was going great and exactly to plan in readiness for the big event.

9- Snap out of It, the Baby's Here

On the 18th August, we welcomed Erin Isabel Thexton into the world. After everything that had happened over the past three years, we had created the most beautiful baby. She was perfect, and not because she looked like me! When I looked at her, straight away I thought to myself, I would never let anything ever harm her and that I would be there and then give my life for her. As I'm sure millions of people around the world feel when they have a baby that their life has changed forever, and my thoughts were no different at this time.

The labour didn't go to plan, I suppose it never does. By the time we realised that it had gone completely the opposite of what we had been taught during our antenatal classes, Erin was already born. By the time I realised Sian was in labour, she was already having strong contractions. I had an iPad and was timing each time she had them and for how long. I called the maternity department at the hospital and said, "She's having contractions every two minutes here, I'm sure she is ready to come in." "No," they said. "She needs to be in labour much longer before she can come in." It was no sooner after that phone call, that I was driving her to the hospital at full pelt, while she screamed from the back seat that she was pushing. "Pant!" "Pant!" I screamed from the driver's seat. These are the breathing techniques we had been taught during our classes. I had to go a different way to the hospital than I would normally because it had speed bumps. I don't think I've heard Sian swear so much in such a short space of time! We arrived at the hospital, me leaving the car right outside the maternity unit.

I rushed her into the maternity ward in a wheelchair, being greeted by the midwife we spoke to on the phone. 'I told you she needed to come in,' I said anxiously to the midwife. Now was probably not the time to say I told you so.

Thirty minutes of gas and air, screaming, swearing and crying (all by me), Erin was born. Sian took it all in her stride, no hassle or fuss. I thought of labour as something much more horrific and painful than what Sian experienced. I think I was in a worse state than her and I didn't have to do anything!

The next couple of weeks were a bit of a blur. It was manic to say the least. We had to get used to having a new addition to the family, as well as seeing to countless visitors, who came almost every day for those two weeks. Me and Sian were a little concerned about Dotty meeting Erin and how she would react. But after getting excited initially, she calmed down and accepted her as part of the family. One evening, we were all sat in the lounge, when I caught myself smiling looking over at Sian. She was asleep, holding a sleeping Erin in her arms and Dotty at her feet. I couldn't have been happier right at that moment. I had my own little family.

I returned to work after paternity leave and continued with it as normal. I still worked as many hours as I had been doing before Erin was born. I was also trying to study at home for my accountancy qualification to try and take some more exams. But I had to stop doing this almost immediately as it was virtually impossible to do at home with Erin.

After a week or so of returning to work, I started to notice that I was having quite powerful episodes of feeling low and anxious. What threw me was that they weren't following the pattern they had done for the previous year or two. I would get them intermittently and it would catch me off guard. It would start with feeling low, then I would become anxious, to the point where I would get into a blind panic and start to feel helpless. I know this cycle as if it were an old friend. The difference this time was when this would happen to me in the past, I would place one of my coping mechanisms in the way. I prepared myself and started to think of ways in which to combat it. The main objective when this happened to me was to make sure nobody in work knew what was going on. In the past, this would tire me out, and I would go home and act normal. The problem I had was that I needed to do this in work, but also do it at home as well, so as not to arouse suspicion with Sian, and give her anything to worry about.

I was getting less sleep, much less than I had previously. I went to bed a bit later than normal as I gave Erin her last bottle. During the night, I was disturbed a couple of times when Sian was up with Erin, and I would wake a little earlier than I would normally, at around 5 am, to give Erin her morning bottle. I'm sure this played a part in it all. I had no reserves of energy to be able to suppress anything anymore.

It was frustrating, because ever since the episode after the night of the 12 week scan, I hadn't really had extreme episodes which I couldn't control.

Keeping it quiet worked OK for a few weeks, but it did tire me out. I didn't know who I was during this time. I had so many different faces. My exterior was showing that there was nothing wrong with me, while inside I was screaming. I would go from feeling happy and content, to extremely sad and depressed within the space of 30 minutes. Something had to give, there was no way I could continue on this path. In the past I was able to pretend in work, then come home and collapse before I ended up lashing out. But I couldn't have that time anymore, I needed to increase the pretence for even longer.

One evening I was walking with Dotty on the field by our house when, all of a sudden, I became light-headed, sweating and dazed. I was looking at Dotty, then looking up at my surroundings, not knowing where I was and what I was doing. It felt similar to the incident I had on the night of Sian's 12 week scan. This time it felt a bit like I was watching myself from afar, watching this all unfold in front of me. It was one of the strangest feelings I have ever had and it really scared me.

I walked back home with Dotty, trying to decipher what had just happened. It certainly isn't concussion this time, I haven't been hit with anything on my head. So what was it? I started to think it was maybe something to do with my accident, something had reared its head after all this time. I started to worry about my state of mind, in particular because I now had Erin. What would happen if something happened to me, I couldn't take care of her, I couldn't help her grow up, helping her with homework and through school.

Again I was faced with the dilemma of telling somebody. I was adamant again that I would not tell Sian or my family, not wanting my condition to dampen anybody's spirits after such a joyful time for our family. But I was getting to the point where I couldn't hide it, and I felt like it was going to come out one way or another if I didn't do something about it. Why was this happening and why were they so strong? I decided that I needed to introduce something new in my life to combat this latest side effect.

I needed to become occupied with something again. So one evening, I was thinking of something which would do the trick and I had an idea. I contacted the company that the family business used for its social media presence and website upkeep and presented them with an idea for a professional genealogy service I wanted to offer people and asked them to set up a website for me. I wanted to offer an affordable genealogy service to people who wished to know about their family history, but had neither the time, nor the inclination to do it. This provided me with a distraction whilst not in work, designing the site and working on how it would function. When it went live, I had a few customers I did family research for (if you want to see it then visit www.tracemyfamilyline.com.)

I also kept myself busy by fully embracing the parent role. I thought that if I kept myself busy, just worrying about my family, making sure Sian, Erin and Dotty were all OK, then my brain would be kept occupied with what was going on.

This provided me with a welcome distraction for a period of time. I was able to keep things at bay for around a month, but it still wasn't enough. The three years of hiding any mental side effects of my brain injury, were slowly starting to rear their ugly head in a variety of different ways. It has been later described to me as a pressure cooker, I had ploughed on ahead with my life, ignoring anything relating to my mental state of mind and ignoring any side effects and giving them a tangible and physical prognosis.

I had always suffered from headaches, usually after a period of anxiety. However, the headaches I was getting now were even stronger. Headaches were the only physical side effect I was getting, aside from fatigue. Nothing seemed to shift them. One day, I was searching in the medicine cupboard for some pain relief when I found some codeine tablets which Sian had been prescribed a while ago. I remember taking codeine when I first came out of hospital and I knew they were quite strong. I took two pills and, within about ten minutes, I felt really relaxed and trouble free. This was the answer, I thought. I started taking these tablets every day, just two in the morning, and this would give me a little boost for the day, and start my day off feeling relaxed.

It was getting to the point where I was just waiting for something to happen, bad or good, where I could attach my anxiety to. I just didn't relax at all, 24 hours a day. I was wired, on alert, all the time. It was no life and it was a miserable way of living. What sort of person sits around waiting for something bad or good to happen? They just happen and you just deal with it at the time. I suppose part of me was thinking about what had happened to me and I didn't want to be caught out again off guard. But you can't live like that and I had gone on feeling like this for way too long.

Looking back now, I feel so sorry for myself, the lengths I took to ensure that nobody knew what was going on inside my head, so as not to worry anybody. I convinced myself that each time I came up with a remedy to combat the stronger side effects I was encountering, it would work.

But it came to a point where even the codeine didn't work. Although they gave me the kick I needed in the daytime, by the time I got to the evening, or towards the end of the week and into the weekend, they couldn't shift my internal distress.

I was completely lost. I had nobody that I could talk to. I didn't even know where to start. Every time that I thought I was ready to confess to Sian, I stopped myself, I can't do this to her. I didn't want to speak to my family about it either. I was a grown man, with my own family, I didn't want to go running to them, telling them I couldn't cope. I also worried about telling them instead of Sian, I should tell her first, not them. This cycle continued over and over again. I became scared of myself, I was worried about what I was thinking, how dark I was becoming, how tired I was becoming trying to pretend I was OK. I tried to speak with my dad in work. There were a few times when I met him in his office and we got talking. It had been on the tip of my tongue to tell him, but I always stopped short, thinking it wasn't the right time. Then one of our phones would go off and it would be forgotten about.

Thinking about it now, Sian was a crutch to me for all those years. She helped me get through some of the worst times in my life, by just being there for me. Even if both of us didn't realise it at the time, she was there for me, to pick up the pieces. With the arrival of Erin, both our priorities had changed within a moment to her. Subconsciously, I must have known that the support network I had for all those years had gone. I could no longer rely on Sian to provide me with support when I needed it. I knew that if I was not feeling great or if I was having a bad day, I could remedy it at home, whilst Sian carried the slack. But that wasn't an option anymore, Sian couldn't carry the slack, she had Erin to care for. I think this scared me, I had nowhere to go, and I couldn't just come home anymore and decide I was having an off day.

I felt like I needed something in the tank for when I got home. I needed to have the energy to be a Dad. But I needed to carry on keeping busy, to keep the demons inside my head at bay. So I had to find the energy from somewhere.

It felt like I was trapped. Trapped in a life I couldn't get out of. It was like being in a prison, screaming the roof down and nobody listening to me. I would hold back, not say anything, and then, just as I was about to say something, something else would happen and all attentions would be drawn to that. I always missed my chance to say something. It was completely my fault, and I was feeling sorry for myself that I was trapped in a life I couldn't cope with anymore.

I decided that enough was enough, I needed help.

10- Help, I Need to Talk to Somebody

It all came to a head one Saturday evening when I was upstairs in our house. I had just started the cycle of the weekend blues and I was in the bedroom, trying to compose myself. I had it really bad this weekend and I was worried that someone would notice what was going on. I couldn't go on like this anymore.

I was readying myself to come out with it. I started the cycle of thinking through in my head what I would say. I was in quite a lot of pain with my headaches and I wasn't really thinking straight at the time. I was exhausted from trying to keep it from everyone. But it was that bad, I couldn't hide it from Sian and I thought I might as well come out with it and tell her everything. I really didn't want to. I had been able to cope this long and get on with my life fine. I knew in my mind that Sian thought I had recovered and we had closed that chapter in our lives long ago. But I was about to open it back up.

Sian was downstairs with Erin. It's not fair on her to tell her now because she was feeding her. I'll wait until tomorrow. I could ask her or my parents to look after Erin for a few hours and then I can tell her. But when will that be? Can I wait until then to tell her? She is going to call up in a minute and I need to get myself together.

On and on I went through this in my head until I finally just decided that I couldn't keep it in any longer so I went and sat on the stairs and called to Sian. She was about to be hit with three and a half years of baggage and I felt so guilty for telling her.

'What's up?' she said. 'There's something I need to tell you,' I said. Sian wasn't completely oblivious to everything that was going on, she was aware that I did suffer from headaches, and was aware that I had changed my personality after my accident. But what I wanted to tell her went much deeper than that.

I went on and explained to her that I had been suffering from periods of feeling low for a few months and that it was getting too much, in particular, my headaches were getting quite severe and I was worried that something was going on with my brain. I hadn't gone lock, stock and barrel with her, but I told her enough for her to decide that I should go to hospital to have it checked out. She called my parents and they came round. Erin had a chest infection at the time, cementing even further my guilt. Sian couldn't come to the hospital with me, she needed to stay with Erin and care for her. I went to the hospital with my mum. I didn't think I really needed to go to hospital, but I was that worried about what was going on, I just wanted somebody to tell me what it was.

I waited for about four hours at the hospital whilst they conducted tests on me. At this point I was convinced in my head that there was something going on physically and I was just waiting for news to confirm this. I had been here before, less than a year ago, when I was told I had suffered concussion. But I was convinced then as I am now, that what I suffered back then wasn't concussion. I was experiencing similar symptoms to those of my previous hospital visit, albeit they were worse now.

Eventually the doctors came to see me. They explained that the scans and other tests they had conducted, showed nothing. So, in terms of anything physically wrong, there wasn't anything. They couldn't tell me what it was. In black and white terms, nothing had shown up, there was nothing to suggest that I was anything other than fully fit. But I knew this wasn't the case.

When I was sat there in the hospital, I almost wanted them to find something, so at least I knew what it was. I was getting frustrated that they couldn't tell me, although I knew it wasn't their fault. There is nothing they can see on the tests they conducted. When I explained what had been happening to me, he suggested that I could be perhaps suffering from a post-traumatic stress after my accident, or that I might just be suffering from high levels of stress, in particular now that I had a baby. He commented that I may have some chemical imbalance in my brain, which needed to be addressed. "That's just a fancy way of saying I was depressed," I thought at the time.

He recommended that I went to my GP, who could put me in touch with a brain rehabilitation service. I didn't even know that a service like this existed, I just thought that there were only services similar to the ones I received leaflets over, which were charities. I didn't really get the answers I wanted, and I was quite frustrated that nobody could tell me what it was. On the way home from the hospital, I said to my mum, 'How can nothing be showing up on the tests? I can't be imagining all these things.'

When I went to my GP, I explained what had been going on. I didn't go into lots and lots of detail, it was such a long winded story, I just wanted to stick to what was happening right now. He told me that medically, there wasn't anything he could suggest. He had read my notes and saw nothing sticking out. This was even more frustrating for me as I knew in my own mind that something was wrong but not even the GP could tell me what it was. He decided to refer me to an acute brain injury service that was based in Chester. They would contact me to arrange an appointment. I had never heard of this service before, but the doctor explained that they would take my case on and provide support for me.

It was really hard going to the doctors, as I've only ever been before when I have had something obvious wrong with me. I was going in now not exactly knowing what it was, but just knew something wasn't right. I couldn't pinpoint a physical side effect other than headaches, and I had been having pain relief for them.

He also prescribed me amitriptyline, which works by balancing the chemicals inside my brain. I took these whilst I waited for my consultation with the acute brain injury service. I had never taken tablets relating to any sort of stress before. I had taken pain relief many times in my life, but I was really reluctant to take any tablets of this type. I had a stigma against such tablets. I thought that they make you into some sort of zombie, unable to function and unable to express any emotions whatsoever. I was assured that this drug in particular just prevented certain things happening in my brain, which would stop the headaches, but nothing much else.

I was advised that I would not notice anything for a while whilst my body got used to them. After a short while, I noticed that my headaches had subsided almost completely. This was great for me and they were crippling me when they came on. I couldn't do anything when I experienced a bad headache.

Although they did work in removing my headaches, I still had all the symptoms I was trying to rid myself of. I was still anxious, feeling panicky and was conscious of my emotions and behaviours. I took these tablets naively thinking that it was some sort of wonder drug that would completely cure me. If only it would have been that simple. I was used to taking pain relief or a course of antibiotics that would clear up any ailment I had. Why couldn't this drug cure me of my current ailment?

I received a letter in the post a few weeks after I went to the GP. It was from the brain injury service. They wanted to come out and speak with me.

A doctor coming to my house? Is it that bad? Why do they need to come all the way to my house to speak with me? At first, I said to Sian, 'I really don't want them coming to my house, they must think I am mad or something and not safe to drive to their clinic.' 'Calm down,' she said, 'it will be fine, it's probably just what they do with everybody.'

I surrendered and let them come to our home, at around the end of November 2015. At this point, I will admit, I was desperate. I just needed help, I needed some answers and ways for me to get rid of what I was going through. It was especially hard, as I had to admit defeat. I had managed this far with my own coping mechanisms, but it had become much stronger than anything I could manage. I needed to do this for Erin, I needed to be OK for her. There was no point in Erin having a Dad that was sick all the time, and unable to care for her. I knew that something needed to be sorted. I was on drugs just to stop the headaches from happening, but even they couldn't stop the roller coaster whizzing round inside my head all the time.

During my initial consultation with the doctor and the case worker, Sian was with me, along with Erin. I explained in detail to them what had been happening to me. I had gone through most things, as much as I could think, during the time they were there. I knew some of it would be hard listening for Sian as she had not heard most of this before. She had heard some of it fleetingly during vulnerable points in the past three and a half years, in particular during our conversation before I went to hospital. I know she would have been annoyed for me leaving it until now to say everything, but, in my mind, I only not told her to protect her. I didn't realise or ever think that I would get to this point. I didn't want to leave any stone unturned.

The doctor and the case worker sat and listened to me for a while. They then came up with an action plan. They immediately said I was suffering from fatigue. As I have explained earlier, I have suffered from fatigue, without realising it, for years. The fatigue was relating to my whole body, brain included. Physical fatigue was making me tired and not wanting to do anything past a certain point. But the mental fatigue was what was making me as bad as I was. I was getting to points in the week, usually towards the end of the week, where I reached a threshold where I just couldn't function properly. The fog would descend over me and I couldn't operate as normal. This is probably what brought on the whole variety of symptoms I was suffering. Probably not the whole reason, but a contributor. It seemed simple at the time to me. Like a eureka moment. But the word "fatigue" means tiredness to a lot of people. But fatigue can get you in many different ways, and I was suffering from mental fatigue primarily.

I also explained to them the behavioural and emotional changes which I had admitted to since my accident. I explained that I had become a bit obsessive since my accident and gave them the same examples I spoke of earlier. I explained that I don't deal with things in the same way, especially if I feel stressed. I lash out when I am stressed, then immediately regret it.

I told them I felt anxious all the time, and felt quite panicky, in particular towards the end of the week and into the weekend. I had gone through the sudden change in everything since Erin was born and how it had gone downhill since then.

The action plan to deal with the fatigue was for me to work less hours, as well as taking frequent naps during the day. This was going to be hard, as I worked full time, with little or no breaks. I would try and come home at dinner time and have a small nap to recharge my batteries. I was also being put on a fatigue management course with other fatigue sufferers. Simple in theory, and I wanted to see how I got on with it.

Regarding the other things we discussed during the consultation, they explained that they would like to discuss them in more detail, but explained that the changes I have seen since my accident are things which I might have to learn to live with and accept. But they can be severely reduced if I managed my fatigue better.

They would return in the next few weeks as they wanted to conduct some tests on me to ascertain my brain function and to see if it was OK.

I was at last trying to deal with it. I knew that it was going to be a long road to get back to normal and to go on living my life normally. As soon as they left, I started to question everything I had done over the past three years. I started thinking to myself, "All this time, when I thought I was dealing with it, was I?" Was I actually happy during this time? I was definitely happy, I had gone through some life changing events and some of the best times of my life. However, the weekend blues which I would get every single week was frustrating, they certainly didn't make me happy. The anxiety and panic that I would have on a weekly basis wasn't making me happy, I only felt happier when I put something in the way to make me take my mind off it. But even then, I was working ridiculously hard, much harder than I needed to, just to feel relatively normal and sane.

Had I just been kidding myself all this time, when, in fact, I was just making things worse? Even though I thought I was doing the right thing in not telling anybody, have I actually made the wrong choice? I had now got into the situation where I was having doctors round at my house, whilst my wife was sat there with Erin.

I started kicking myself. If I'd have known it was fatigue causing this then I would have just dealt with it then. But the problem was I didn't know it was fatigue. I didn't feel fatigued, I just felt like there was something wrong with me because I couldn't operate properly. I couldn't define what it was. I had never even heard of fatigue in that context before. I never appreciated until then what your brain has to do and how much energy it requires just for you to function normally on a daily basis. I can just imagine my brain, as I approached the weekend, just switching off completely. I thought back to the countless weekends where I would wake up on a Saturday morning and just explode as soon as me and Sian had exchanged morning pleasantries and discussed our plans for the weekend.

I started thinking about my obsessiveness and the repetitiveness which followed me everywhere. Once I approached the weekend, it was uncharted waters. I hated the fact that nothing was planned out for me and it was open for discussion. Every Saturday morning I would speak with Sian and talk about the weekend and, if we didn't come up with a plan for the entire weekend, then we would end up in a blazing row. I just couldn't function properly if the entire weekend wasn't planned out for me.

But I didn't know how to deal with that. The doctor said as much to me. I needed to learn to live with things like this, as they were a side effect of what had happened to me. But it was a miserable way of being, having everything planned out so I could feel happier. There isn't much room for manoeuvre then is there?

But I knew I had to give this a go, at least for Erin's sake. So I started taking the tablets, which helped, as well as trying to manage my fatigue. I certainly couldn't deal with any of the anxiety and panic I was going through, but the doctors said that if I tried to manage my fatigue a bit more, then I should notice a reduction in the side effects.

A few weeks passed and I did start to feel a lot better. I was combating the fatigue, which was only a new thing to me then, but it started to make more and more sense. The more I started to ask myself questions, the more I started to question the old tactics I used, the more I understood what was going on. It was as if I had been running away for all this time, and I had suddenly turned around and confronted what was chasing me. Slowly but surely I did start feeling better. At least I now had the energy to combat the anxiety and panic. Rather than "keeping busy" all the time, some of the time I would just rest. I would try and listen to some music and go to sleep. I would leave work early and rest. I would try a whole variety of different techniques to recharge my batteries, giving me enough energy to be relatively normal and function OK.

We were fast approaching the festive period, which would be Erin's first Christmas. Both me and Sian were excited for this, as well as both being happy in the progress I was making. I had been visited by the doctors again, who checked up on how I was dealing with my fatigue. They had given me some more tips to deal with everything and hopefully I should see some further improvements over time. I was to start the fatigue management class in the New Year as well which was something for me to look towards.

I felt as though I was at last turning a corner, after everything that I had been through. I had finally admitted to myself, as well as to my family, that I had problems I needed to deal with, for the sake of my own health, but also my happiness. I wasn't living any sort of life, hiding from things and hoping they would go away. I wasn't thriving or becoming a better person, I was just treading water, hoping that it would eventually go away.

Leaving work for the Christmas holiday, I remember driving home in my car, thinking to myself, "2016 will be a good year for us, I can finally put all this behind me and start to live my life and be happy."

Unfortunately for me and my family, life would not be that simple.

11- Boxing Night

I celebrated my 28th birthday on Boxing Day 2015. We went to my parents' new house, joined by many friends and family. During the evening, Sian had taken Erin home and I stayed out for an extra hour to have a drink in the local pub with a few of my cousins, my brother Tom, my uncle and my friend Mia. Everyone was in good spirits. I was happy to be celebrating my birthday, but sad that I was another year older! After a short while, Mia was picked up and she dropped me off at my house. Sian was in bed and Erin was in bed next to her. We sat up, Sian asking me how the pub was. 'Yeh, it was OK, I only had a couple of drinks. Tom and Matthew,' (my uncle) 'had moved on to another pub and I was getting tired so I came home with Mia.' Sian asked why I didn't go out with them two, but I couldn't really be bothered having anymore to drink and staying out any longer. I could count on one hand the amount of times I had been out late in the past couple of years, maybe I was getting too old for it.

I was more excited to spend the remainder of my Christmas break relaxing, getting plenty of sleep, spending time with Sian and Erin and getting ready for my treatment in the New Year. It is quite surreal now to think about me going to bed that night, after spending all day with my family and coming home happy and content, not knowing what was about to unfold.

At about 5 am I was woken up. I was stirring around in my bed and I thought that perhaps Erin had woken up. When I opened my eyes I saw that my phone was ringing by the side of my bed and it was my dad. I instantly knew something was going on.

'What's going on?' I said. 'Don't panic, it's OK. Tom has been in an accident and he's in hospital with a fractured skull.' My heart sank, I knew it was serious by the way my dad told me this whilst sobbing. I didn't know any more than that. Sian was awake at this time, Erin was next to us in her Moses basket, sleeping peacefully, unaware that both her parents were awake. 'What's up?' Sian said. 'It's Tom. He's in hospital, he's fractured his skull.' Sian was asking me more questions, but I didn't know the answers. I ended the call quickly with my dad and didn't ask any more.

I immediately got in my car and drove as fast as I could to the hospital. I was met by my mum and dad who were outside crying and I spoke to them before going in to see Tom. He was in the A&E department of a hospital, overseen by The Walton Centre, the brain hospital which we had all spent so much time in just three years previous.

He was in hospital clothes, lying lifeless in the Resus area of the hospital. I thought at the time that to look at him, you wouldn't think anything was wrong, he just looked asleep. He didn't have any marks on his face, or his body. The fracture that he had was behind his right ear, so you couldn't see the damage. It was very surreal to see him there. He had all sorts of machines next to him.

When I came out from seeing him I went over to my mum and dad. They weren't sure what had happened to him. Dad explained that he received a call at about 4 am from a policeman who had activated Tom's Siri on his iPhone and said, "Call Dad." The policeman said that he had been found lying in the road unconscious and that an ambulance was called. When we spoke to the police, they couldn't provide us with much information, other than what they knew from the ambulance driver, who reported that an ambulance was called from someone who claimed Tom was lying in the road, with nobody knowing what had happened to him. This made it so much worse, thinking of Tom, lying there with no help, on his own. It's one thing him being in hospital in a bad way, it's another not actually knowing what had happened to him, that's what hurt the most.

We waited for what seemed like an eternity for the doctors to come and explain to us what they were going to do. When they did finally come they explained that Tom was brought to the hospital and was unconscious. He had slowly come round at hospital but was not responsive to anything they asked so they have re-sedated him. They explained that due to the location of his injury and the fracture, they wanted to induce a coma and transfer him to The Walton Centre intensive care unit and have him monitored there.

I cannot imagine how my parents felt at this time. For both their sons within the space of three and a half years to both be in comas, at the same hospital, both facing life threatening conditions, it was like a crazy déjà vu moment. For me, it was like looking at myself all those years ago, in exactly the same situation Tom faced himself. He was lying there, like I was, completely unaware. It was strange in a way, all of us in pieces over what was going to happen, whilst I knew that Tom would be in dreamland, without a care in the world.

Everything that my family told me about when I was in hospital, all resonated in this moment with me. All the things that I couldn't appreciate at the time, the waiting round, not knowing what was going to happen, being surrounded by nurses and doctors in the A&E department, with Tom, just lying there, lifeless. It was very early in the morning as well, people wouldn't even be awake after Boxing Night, after the family occasion we had less than twelve hours later. Little did they know what they were waking up to.

Entering the hospital for the first time in three years was haunting. I never thought that I would return to this place again, if I did, it would be under completely different circumstances. Tom was to be moved immediately into Intensive Care.

We entered the family room, such a familiar place to my family. The first thing my dad said was, "Here we go again." This family room which I had heard so much about from my family, I was actually here. Such a little insignificant room, I thought, with just a few sofas, a TV and a small kitchen. As I walked in, I could see people had left Christmas cards and small gifts. Inside one of the cards it read, "Wishing you a very happy Christmas during this difficult time for you and your family. We hope that your loved one makes a full recovery. We didn't get a happy ending, but we hope that you do." That struck me instantly, that someone who had obviously lost someone here would write a card for families that they had not even met before.

I never spent any time in the family room at the hospital so I couldn't empathise with either of my parents as to how they felt and what they had gone through whilst in this room during my stay at the hospital. I would soon come to understand the emotional roller coaster that you have whilst spending time in this room, made even worse that it was Christmas, which made it all the more surreal.

To be honest it felt as though I was dreaming, it just felt so surreal. How could this be happening to our family again? You just wouldn't believe it.

We sat in silence in the family room, shell shocked at what had happened to Tom. This silence was ended by a knock on the door. In came two doctors asking for next of kin. Mum and Dad said that me and my sister could sit in, so we listened nervously to what they were about to say.

They said that from the injury he had sustained to his head, it seemed as though he had fallen from a standing position onto the back of his head, suggesting that he had not broken his fall, which was conducive to being knocked out. He didn't have any injuries on his body apart from the fracture in his skull and he had suffered a subarachnoid haemorrhage and there was a bleed on his brain. They wanted to monitor his brain whilst he was under and then try and wake him. He was in a critical position and they didn't have any more information for us right at that time but they would monitor him regularly and update us if necessary.

While we were worried about the welfare of Tom, it made it more a bitter pill knowing that he was, more than likely, knocked out by someone or something, and had been left on the road unconscious. That made me sick to my stomach. I started thinking about what I was doing only 12 hours previously. I was sat in a pub with him, laughing and joking. I remember him talking about going out and I wasn't interested at all in coming with him. I tried to think of the last words I said to him, I couldn't remember them.

It was one thing coming back into the hospital for the first time, but nothing could prepare me for what I felt going back into the Intensive Care Department. As I walked in, I was hit by a mixture of different sensations. The first thing that got me was the smell. It wasn't a smell which you recognise as an everyday smell, it was a hospital smell. I almost wanted to walk straight back out and never come back. But that wasn't an option.

As I got closer to Tom's bed, the next thing that got me was the noise. The noise of the machines in particular and the constant beeping and alarm sounds. They seemed so much louder than I thought, it felt as though I couldn't hear anybody talking, they were that loud in my ear.

There were so many doctors and nurses on the ward. They all seemed so busy, caring for different patients. I started to have flashbacks, remembering parts of the room and the different areas. This was placed in my dreams all those years ago, under a completely different setting.

I would say that entering that ward for the first time was one of the weirdest things I have ever gone through in my life. I have never been a really emotional type of person, but right at that time, all I wanted to do was break down. To look at me though, I was emotionless. I had been a master of disguises and keeping things from people. This time more than any other I had ever faced, I was not going to tell anybody about what was going on. There was just no way that I could make this about me.

Nothing entered my thought process about the discussions I'd had with the brain injury team only weeks previous. They had explained to me about opening up and talking to people. But there's one thing suggesting it, but there's another doing it in practice. When your parents and your sister are in visible distress after what had happened, I couldn't stand there and say, "I know this is a bad time, but I am not really coping being in here." There was no way they could tell me how to deal with this, you couldn't even make this up, it was that far-fetched.

12- Tom's Turn

As we approached the room where Tom was for the first time, he was assuming the same position where I saw him only a few hours previously. He was lying on his back, albeit with more machines attached to him this time. As I walked into the room, one of the nurses that was looking after him said to me, "Have you been here before?" Our surname is quite unique so they recognised it straight away. They couldn't believe that a member of the same family was here so soon after what had happened to me.

They couldn't really tell us any more than we had already been told a few hours ago. They were just monitoring him all the time, trying to keep him stable. He wasn't in any position to be woken up or anything else done with him at this time.

Walking out of the ward, leaving him for the first time, I kept myself occupied by trying to work out what had happened to him. I was trying to go through different scenarios in my head. I contacted people I knew that might have been out that night to see if they saw what happened. Everywhere I turned I hit a dead end. Surely someone knew what happened to him?

During the course of the next few days however, the police continued their inquiries, shutting the road off where he was found and checking CCTV. We had a meeting with them a few days later, and they were able to confirm what had happened. My mum's sister, who came down from Yorkshire to help, was a policewoman and she carried out a few enquiries on our behalf as well to try and help.

Tom was trying to enter a nightclub and ended up arguing with the bouncer on the door. At some point during this argument, Tom was struck at the back of the head by the bouncer, knocking him out and his head hitting the kerb on the roadside. Once he had fallen, somebody ran into the nightclub, presumably to call an ambulance, whilst somebody else put Tom into the recovery position and sat with him until the ambulance came. The first thought that went through my head was how did the ambulance crew not know what had happened? If it was as clear as that on CCTV then why were we only given small pieces of information on the night of the accident? This got me annoyed thinking about it. I started thinking that someone wasn't honest with the ambulance driver and Tom was sent to hospital, with the nurses and doctors not knowing exactly what injuries he had. I thought that perhaps they could have saved him from being put into a coma or they could have done something different.

Even though this was going round and round in my head, and as difficult as it was to hear what the police had to say, we were still in the position we were in and nothing would change that. My parents weren't really interested in what had happened to Tom, they were only concerned for his welfare.

Luckily for us, the fundraising that we contributed to over twelve months previous for a respite centre for families, meant that there was somewhere we could stay overnight. At least we didn't have to sleep on the floor, like my family had to do when I was here. At least we could be close to Tom and be in a warm bed. Considering the circumstances, the rooms were really nice and the "Home From Home" appeal which helped build it had done a great job.

If anybody has had to spend any time in any hospital waiting rooms, sitting with other families who are equally as worried about their loved ones, then you will understand how strange it is in there. Times like this bring out the best and the worst in people and I saw all of these emotions during my time there. For me, I always felt on the periphery of the family room, I almost felt like a fraud and that I didn't belong. I had been on the other side of this only recently and, whilst many people in that room received bad news every day, I and my family had been lucky and I was back to rub it in. That's how I felt anyway.

I would see people looking at me and talking, knowing that they were talking about my previous stay in the hospital. It didn't really bother me all that much, in a way, it's a good thing as it gives people hope that you can come through something like this and come out the other end with a decent life after it. The other side of me was thinking, everybody in there is really not well and everybody's brains work differently after trauma. So just because my brain recovered, doesn't mean that everybody else's brains would recover the same.

This was the same for my family as well, although being here again must have been the hardest thing they have ever had to deal with. I knew they were thinking, well, we have been here before and we got through it, which is great. But then they were also thinking, Ben came through, and Tom is made of similar stuff and he will pull through.

There were up to 20 people at any one time in this family room, people from all walks of life, all huddled together with a collective aim of being there for their loved one. This family room was exclusive to people in intensive care or high dependency, so 99% of their loved ones were very, very critical. Some of the stories you heard, considering the festive time of the year, in any other circumstances you would break down and cry, but that wasn't an option. There was one couple who were from Bristol who travelled to the Lake District for a short break away and the husband had suffered a severe stroke. There was another lady from Wales that suffered some sort of brain haemorrhage whilst the husband was out. There was a young man who fell down some stairs and hit his head against a radiator. There were countless other people as well with similar stories, all sat in one room. Just taking one day at a time, it would be enough to scar you for life, but there must have been about ten different families in there with equally harrowing stories.

103

How do people deal with what's going on? How would you react to something as drastic as what was unfolding with not just our family, but countless other families in the same position?

I think that times like these tend to bring the best and worst out in people. There were people bringing in food and drink for people to share. They would ask after each and every one of the family members, checking to see if they had any progress. There were families which had a lot of visitors, and they sat and talked most of the day. There were people that would spend all day in the family room, not once going into the ward to see their loved one. They were probably scared stiff of what they would see.

There was one family in particular that I remember, who would constantly complain about the parking charges in the hospital. It made me laugh in a way, because I'm sure that if you could, you would give up everything for your loved one to be OK, yet there they were, complaining about the price of parking! I suppose that's how they dealt with it and maybe it took their minds off what was going on.

The way in which our family in particular dealt with Tom was, according to Sian who was at home with our baby, a carbon copy of last time. My dad didn't leave the hospital the entire time. My mum struggled to be sat in the family room and it got too much, even more so after being here for the second time. My sister and her boyfriend were at the hospital and taking care of the animals at my parents' house. We were also visited most days by Tom's best friend Sam, who was on school holidays as he was a primary school teacher. We had daily visiting from friends and family as well. The only difference here was that I was replacing Tom in the equation.

During this time, how I dealt with this was by just getting on with it. Every time I saw anybody crying, both from my family and from other people in the family room, I got annoyed. I thought to myself, this isn't going to help. Both our and your loved ones are in there, fighting for their lives, so we have to fight alongside them.

That said, the cynic in me was thinking that they are completely out of it anyway and are unaware of where they are and who is around them. Visiting them and spending all day, every day in the family room is cathartic for you but it won't change the outcome of their recovery.

It's therapeutic for you as you feel as though you are going through it with them, step by step, and you are there in case something happens. The emotional side in my brain was never the same anyway after my accident, but it was really put to the test in this situation. But all I could think about at the time was to just get on with it.

At night I would go home and see Sian, Erin and Dotty, and spend time with them, before starting it all again the next day. There were nights I spent with my dad in the family rooms adjacent to the hospital, but I didn't want to spend too much time away from my family. I didn't go home and vent off to Sian, I just tried to take my mind off what had happened that day, otherwise I would have gone mad. Going home, I felt guilty. I felt guilty leaving Tom, I felt guilty leaving Dad on his own in the hospital, but I felt guilty leaving Sian at home on her own with Erin and Dotty. We had planned to do so much with the time I had off over Christmas. But Sian understood where I needed to be and I felt comfortable knowing that at least home was OK with Sian looking after everything.

During the days in the hospital, I would spend as much time as I could on the ward. There were visiting times that people stuck to, but I would chance my luck any time I could. There were quite a few nurses that had treated me when I was here, so many of them would let me in and sit with Tom.

I would just sit there for hours and hours, watching his monitors. I became familiar with what different things meant, I knew what sedation he was on, the current levels he was on when I left, then what they had changed to when I came back. The stronger the sedation, the longer it takes for someone to wake up basically. The strongest sedation he was on was call Rocuronium which effectively paralysed him. So if I saw that being pumped into him, that means they wanted him more deeply sedated.

I also checked his ventilator. I knew that every couple of hours, they would check his blood oxygen levels and, depending on the results, this would determine how much support he needed. At many times during the second week, he was on 100% oxygen, which means that he can't receive any more support than he is currently getting. I think this was my way of coping with it all. Being in the thick of it meant I was kept occupied. I got it into my head that I needed to know everything about what was going on, what every drug meant, what every beep meant, so as to not miss anything. I thought in my head, if I know everything about what is going on then I won't be surprised. I would have been driven mad if I stayed in the family room all day not knowing what was going on and how he was doing.

As I said previously, during these times, I didn't think of anything other than Tom. You do not think of yourself whatsoever. I was thinking of my parents though. I wanted to try and remember as much information I heard as possible, so they knew what was going on. I knew that my mum didn't like being in the room with Tom, so I would try and tell her as much information as I can. Sometimes, I think I said too many things, but I didn't want to keep anything back. I was almost like a messenger at times!

When I was with him, it did dawn on me how this must have been for me when I was here. How serious it all was. I don't know whether it was a good thing me seeing all this stuff and going through it all the other way round this time. Your brain and your body aren't used to being in the situation Tom is in, so it's certainly not used to seeing it unfold before your eyes. It was a confusing time as I wasn't sure of my feelings at this time. All I was clear on, was what I needed to do to help my family and Tom, and, at the same time, keeping myself from over thinking things too much by making sure I was in the thick of things as much as possible. I did get over the initial shock of being in the ward for the first time, and I managed quite well to come in and out as frequently as possible.

Over the course of the week, Tom became more and more unstable. As we moved into the second week, Tom's lungs just decided that they didn't want to work anymore. He had fluid on his lungs which caused an infection and, as well as this, his lungs were fighting being artificially ventilated. We were in a vicious circle, you had his lungs not working, but you also had his brain being swollen and needing time to heal. Tom had a similar device to what I had, which measured the inter-cranial pressures in his head. The more this rose, the more it could cause any further brain damage. Tom coughing and clearing his chest of the infection would send his pressures sky high, which the doctors did not want, meaning that he needed to be more heavily sedated. The more heavily sedated Tom became, the longer he would be under, the more his lungs didn't like it and the worse his chest would become as he couldn't clear it. We just did not know which way to turn at this point. We didn't know what would happen next. We were on a vicious cycle.

One night during the second week, me and my dad spoke to a doctor for a good half an hour in the room with Tom and she explained that his lungs were still unresponsive and that the ventilator was working flat out to keep his body fed with oxygen. She was cautious with us but explained that they were hoping for an improvement in his condition. She just said that they would need to try and keep him as relaxed as possible for a few more days and let the infection leave his body and hopefully his lungs would start working better.

That night we left, relatively happy with the chat we had had with the doctor. My dad left for the first time and went home with my mum and sister. I left to go home to my family. We at least had some direction as to where this was all going. We had set aside the worries about Tom's brain and replaced it with the problems with his chest. But we knew that as long as they could clear his chest, they could continue with his treatment and try and wake him.

As I went through the door I was sat eating my tea, trying to wind down after another day in the hospital. I turned on the TV and tried to unwind. Sian had been to my parents to take Erin round and she called me to say that the hospital had been on to my dad and he just left all of a sudden. I got that gut wrenching feeling again in my stomach.

No sooner had I put the phone down to Sian, I got a call from my dad. He said that the hospital had called him to say that Tom had become extremely unstable in the past couple of hours since we left and he was now extremely critical. I just put the phone down, put on my coat and drove to the hospital. I was met by my dad, shortly followed by my mum and sister.

A neurosurgeon had been called in from home to deal with Tom and he called us into a side room. He explained that Tom's oxygen levels had dropped progressively over the past few hours and that he was on the maximum support that they could give him. 'We are doing everything we can for Tom, but his body is just rejecting everything we are trying to do,' said the doctor. We weren't sure what this meant for Tom, we were trying to read between the lines. I think the doctor knew what we were thinking.

"He could die," was the next sentence from the doctor which hit us all really hard. That's how bad it was. It was a hard thing to hear and it made my stomach do somersaults. When someone is suffering from head trauma, you are immediately concerned with the welfare of their brain, forgetting that to get the brain stable and reduce any swelling, you need to effectively turn the body off and leave it to machines. But it's not that easy, especially if your body does not like being told what to do, which, in this case, is what Tom's body decided to do. You prepare yourself for the worst anyway when you are in this situation. But you run the different scenarios through your head, all of which, for me anyway, included brain damage. I never once thought that something other than his brain would put him in danger of dying. But that's what was happening to Tom.

"The only thing left for us to do is to make him prone. It is quite dangerous considering the pressures it will cause to Tom's brain, but we have no choice given the circumstances." Tom was being moved onto his belly (prone) in a last ditch attempt to increase the air in his lungs. Although there was a risk of what the doctor called "secondary brain damage", we didn't care, we just didn't want him to die.

As we left the room, everyone broke down in tears, completely hysterical after the news he had given us all. Everyone was really downbeat and, even though we were in the situation we were in, we weren't prepared for what he told us. If we weren't prepared for the fact that Tom might die from this, then this definitely put all our minds into that way of thinking.

Whilst all this is going on, all I can think in my head is that this isn't the time for crying, there is still hope and if there is hope then we fight alongside him. I know this probably sounds crazy and I should have been crying with my parents and my sister, but I just didn't think that way. All I wanted to do was go in and sit with him.

I went straight into the intensive care unit and sat down next to him, shortly followed by my dad. He went over to his bed, whilst he was lying face down. He spoke into his ear, "Tom, if you can hear me, fight this for me, all you need to do is breathe." My sister then came in with Tom's friend Sam, then they all left to get some sleep.

I couldn't sleep. I was scared in case anything happened to him during the night. I wanted to be there, taking it step by step. I stayed with him all night, watching his ventilator and waiting for his bloods to be taken for updates. Usually they are done every four hours, but they were done almost every hour during the night. Every beep of the machine, every alarm sounding, sent me into a panic.

Tom's situation improved slightly overnight. It was probably the most difficult night of my life. Being sat there with your brother, knowing that at any minute he could die is something I wouldn't want to wish on anyone. By the time the morning came, his oxygen levels were good enough for him to be put back on his back. He was out of danger in as much as he could be put on his back and his brain pressures could be kept stable. We were happier, certainly happier than we were the night before, but the doctors and the nurses caring for him explained that he was only "slightly better" than he was last night and that he still remained extremely critical. We still had to wait for Tom to start working by himself and not rely on the life support so much.

Tom couldn't be woken without an additional brain scan, but he couldn't be moved to the scanner as he was so unstable. So we waited, and waited, for his breathing to improve. It went up and down for the next two days until, finally, they were happy for him to go for a scan. The scan came back showing that the swelling on his brain had been reduced which we were very happy with.

That afternoon he would be left to rest and hopefully the day after they would attempt to wake him. "Well, at least the first obstacle is out the way," I thought to myself. We just had to deal with whatever we were left with when Tom woke up. That night, we were all really nervous about what tomorrow would bring. Tom's breathing could still not improve enough for him to be woken, and, even if they were happy for him to be woken, would he be OK?

The doctors explained to us that afternoon that if Tom was woken and his breathing wasn't great, then they would need to fit a tracheostomy into his neck so a tube could be inserted into his windpipe to help him breathe. I have seen one of these fitted before to my grandad when he was in hospital and it's not great as they cannot speak whilst it's attached.

We had gone from one crisis to another now. We now had to deal with what happened when he woke. There was every chance that he might not wake up. He might not be ready or able to wake up and he might need further time asleep.

Not only that but he might wake up brain damaged. To be honest, we had been through that much over the past week, I didn't really care if he was brain damaged or not. I remember speaking with my dad saying, "I don't care anymore if he is brain damaged, as long as he's alive we can just look after him, at least he will be alive."

The morning after came and we tried a few times to get in to see him but we were refused as they were busy with him. We guessed, or hoped, that they were trying to wake him. We waited for a long time, usually we can at least go in and see him and see what they are doing with him that day. It seemed strange that they wouldn't let us in. I convinced myself that they were waking him up because if anything bad had happened, then they would have been in to speak with us by now.

I was sat by the family room door, watching any movement from the Intensive Care doors, watching to see if anybody came out and in our direction.

I went and sat back down in the family room, we were all sat around, not knowing what was going on. The doctor who we met only a few days previous explaining Tom's lung problems, came in to the family room. We all held our breath, waiting for him to call out Tom's next of kin. He just said, "The parents of Tom?" My mum and dad acknowledged him cautiously.

"Tom's awake and asking for you."

After everything that had gone on for those two weeks, he was finally awake and asking for mum and dad. The feeling you get when you hear that is like no other. It was almost as if the doctor had spoken in slow motion.

We all rushed in to see him. After seeing him lifeless for two weeks, he was now sat up with an oxygen mask attached to his face. He still had quite a large amount of sedatives in his system and he was not all there whatsoever, but I could tell it was him, I could tell by the scowl he had on his forehead, he was alright. I knew what he would be thinking when he woke up. I knew that he wouldn't be able to make sense of everything that had happened. I knew that all he would have needed at that moment was to see some friendly faces to at least calm him down and that everything was going to be OK. I knew that he wouldn't have a clue what was going on, that he wouldn't make sense of anything right now, but that didn't matter right at this time.

Tom was dazed and confused for about three days. He wasn't really making much sense as it took a while for the drugs to leave his system. He still had a slight chest infection so he was coughing quite a bit. Eventually though, Tom started to come round and started acting relatively normal. He started asking what had happened and why he was where he was. There was nothing visibly wrong with him both physically and mentally. I knew that Tom would be OK.

Tom was going to be moved onto a ward in a few days' time. My mum in particular was with him a lot, making sure that he was eating and drinking enough and getting enough sleep.

A couple of days after he was awake, we brought Erin in to see Tom. He was wheeled into the family room by the nurse looking after him, and he sat there, holding her for a while. It's very surreal to see your brother, fresh out of a coma, holding your six month old baby, in a waiting room of a hospital.

I sat in the family room after about three days of Tom being awake and just started feeling as though I wanted to go home. I couldn't think of anything worse than going back into Intensive Care and sitting with him. He was being looked after now by mum and dad. I felt as though I had done my job, I had been there for them when they needed me, but now Tom was awake, I thought that he was going to be OK, so all I wanted to do then was go home and back to my family.

I guess that the adrenaline that I was living off whilst he was in intensive care had left my body. It had definitely taken a toll on me, more than I could ever realise. I didn't at that time appreciate how much this would affect me mentally, to be subjected to the same experiences that my family had been through with me. I wanted to be at home after feeling so guilty in leaving Sian, Erin and Dotty. Erin was only six months old and she needed her dad. She wouldn't understand why I wasn't there but I wanted to be with her and spend time with her. All of it wasn't fair. It wasn't fair what happened to Tom and it wasn't fair that Erin had to spend over two weeks without her dad being around.

I had spent months trying to reverse the damage I had caused myself by bottling things up and not telling people anything, but I had definitely taken a few steps back in the past couple of weeks as there was no one really I could speak to during this time. Even if I had wanted to, I spent all my time at the hospital with Tom.

Driving home that afternoon, I was singing along to whatever song it was on the radio, I was so happy that Tom was awake and OK. I was happy that I was now able to return to my family full time and try and get back on with my life. I had taken some steps back in my own personal battle this past couple of weeks, but I thought that I could at least try and get back on course and start being happy again.

At the very least, I thought because of what happened to Tom, our family would be brought even closer together, and that I would be able to help Tom in ways in which I wasn't helped when I was left in the same situation last time.

13- Life Can Resume

Tom was discharged from hospital about a week after he was woken up. He lived at home with my parents so at least they could keep an eye on him and make sure he is OK. He wasn't able to do anything really, as they had banned him from driving for at least three months as he was a seizure risk after his injury. Luckily for Tom, shortly after returning home, he received a letter from the acute brain injury team from Chester, the same people that I was currently dealing with.

I was really pleased that Tom was getting the support straight away, the support which I was crying out for all those years. They had called up when I was at the hospital and Sian had informed them of what was going on. I don't know if they would have been able to reach out to Tom if they didn't already know what was going on. If that was true, then I was pleased that me facing up to my problems and seeking help, had indirectly meant that Tom got the support he needed as soon as he left hospital.

One thing that I ended up doing which I regret now is comparing things with Tom. He was new to all the things he was going through and what it would take out of him. I would say things to him like, "you will end up feeling like this," or "this will happen next." It wasn't the right thing to do. Tom is completely different to me, he had a completely different injury and would deal with it completely differently. I thought at the time that I was helping him, by preparing him for what I thought was going to happen. In hindsight, I shouldn't have said anything like that to him, I should have just been there and supported him with whatever happened next. I couldn't predict how he would react or what his recovery would be like. I thought to myself that the best thing to do would be to take a back seat and let Tom deal with it his way. I didn't want him to look at me and try and compare himself to me as well.

Just because I did things one way, didn't mean that Tom would do the same. I did things in completely the opposite way of what I should have been doing, so I really needed to look at myself first before giving advice. I didn't want Tom to look at what I did and try and follow suit, because I did it wrong, it did me no good. I stopped myself almost straight away when I realised that I was giving out advice to him when I shouldn't have been doing.

Whilst Tom was in hospital, I had ignored all communication with the brain injury team, I think they knew they had to just leave me to it until I was ready to start again. But now that Tom was home and on the road to recovery, I knew that I had to dust myself down to carry on and fight what was going on inside my head, for me, for my family and, most important of all, Erin.

My parents had to deal with Tom, he was their priority, so I wanted to do it for them as well, so as not to be thinking and worrying about me when they had Tom to deal with as well. They knew what was going on with me at the time, but whilst they cared for Tom, I wanted them to know that I was sorting it out for myself.

After a couple of weeks I was visited by the doctors, who wanted to conduct some tests on me. These were the tests which would determine if I had any problems with my brain function. It was a series of tests which happened over a couple of weeks. They were similar to IQ tests, but involved practical elements to them, as well as requiring me to think logically. Some of the questions involved me remembering a shopping list which was read out to me, then trying to remember all the items on the list. Then the next question would be, name the items on the shopping list that are stationery items. Another question involved me remembering the position of counters on a noughts and crosses board then, once the doctor had covered it over, I had to place counters in the same position as what I had just seen. These were the types of questions I had and, at the end, I thought to myself that I had done quite well and was quite confident that I had done OK and wouldn't, I thought, have anything to worry about. I was obsessed with doing well on these tests. I'm a competitive person naturally so I wanted to make sure I had good results!

I think the doctors knew there was nothing wrong with my brain function, they just wanted to conduct some tests to confirm it. They had admitted it themselves when they came out the first time to see me. The problems I was having were my emotional reactions, my obsessiveness, the repetitiveness, and the anxiety and panic. I was hoping that the next stage would help to battle these.

I had received a confirmed date for the fatigue management group. I had reservations about going to this sort of group. As I have said earlier, I've not been the type of person who would sit in a group and open up in front of strangers. I did start to understand fatigue a bit better and I knew there were different types of fatigue. But I thought it was going to be a group of people talking about being tired and then going for a nap. I thought I had it all sussed out before I even went.

Me and Sian both said to each other that I should go with an open mind. I needed to be honest with myself. The techniques that I had been using have obviously not worked so I need to be open to suggestions. These were professional health care people, they would know a lot more about how I can deal with what I was going through better than I could. I just had to put my prejudices to one side and open up for once in my life.

When I walked into the place which held the group, I saw people sat round a table. As I approached, I noticed that a lot of the people were much older than me, and I immediately felt a bit of a fraud.

They all had dealt with a variety of different injuries, relating from strokes, brain haemorrhages and traumatic brain

116

injuries such as mine. I was, at the time, three and a half years post-accident so I was entering this process quite late. They were still all coming to terms with what had happened to them, and having to live with all the side effects. They were all new to this and I felt sorry for them. But at the same time, they were the smart ones, getting support straight away rather than not doing anything about it.

The stuff we spoke about was mainly with each other, as we shared our experiences at dealing with fatigue and living with a brain injury. We commented on how difficult it was for people, in particular, family and friends, to understand what you were going through and how it felt for us to go through it. We spoke about how we managed our problems, the different techniques which we had used. They all had some difficulties in being understood by people, in wanting to open up to loved ones, but feeling hesitant as they thought they didn't understand. It surprised me how similar this all sounded. Although this was specifically for people with brain injuries and fatigue management, the side effects of feeling anxious and depressed is something which I am sure many people suffer with. Although so many people suffer with it, it's still not understood very much, there is a stigma attached to it. I think because it's not a physical symptom, it's something that goes on inside your head, which you need to articulate to people what your symptoms are and how you feel. If you are not very good at articulating what it is, or don't want to tell anybody, then you can be mistaken for being miserable or lazy. It's a shame, I thought at the time that this illness which so many people suffer from isn't widely appreciated or recognised.

For the first session, I didn't really speak. I was analysing the room, I could feel myself looking at each person in the group and weighing up whether I was comfortable opening up in front of them. When they spoke openly, I did resonate with what they were saying and I wanted to speak out and agree with them and share my experiences, but I held back.

One session, I just came out with something. I didn't mean to speak, and I tried to stop myself, but by that time, the room had gone quiet and they all started looking at me.

I started talking about Tom. I explained how I was really struggling with what had happened to him. What I was really finding difficult is that I knew the journey he would need to take. Although what happened to us was completely different, there are still some similarities to it all. 'Tom will sooner or later need to accept what has happened,' I said, 'and that's the hardest part of it all.' I could already see Tom now, carrying on with life regardless and something would have to give eventually, because it's not as easy as that. I know how difficult it is. How do you cope with something like this? Well, a good starting point is carry on with life like you did before and hopefully you get back into the same routine. But I knew it wasn't as simple as that and I found it really difficult watching him going through it. I couldn't really do anything about it because he would need to work it out for himself. I would have been a hypocrite as well, as I did exactly the same thing. I was in doubt as to what I needed to do next, so I reverted to type and did exactly what I was doing before my accident.

After listening to me for a short while, one of the people in the group said, "Tom is a grown man and he will work it out for himself. The best thing for Tom is that you are in the right frame of mind to help him if he has a problem. Tom couldn't be in a better place right now given the circumstances, as he can seek advice from someone who has dealt with it first-hand." They were right. I could do something about it. I was getting myself frustrated because there was nothing I could do. But speaking with the people in the group made me realise that I was trying to impose myself on his recovery, whereas I am best just being there when he asks and offer my advice.

As I attended more and more sessions, I didn't start to feel alone anymore, I felt as though I was with friends, with people who could understand what it felt like and the more I sat and spoke with this group, the more I kicked myself at how naive and pig headed I had been for all these years when I scoffed at this sort of thing. I would come out of every session a stone lighter, as I got more and more off my chest. Although I could speak to people about it at home, it wasn't the same, when I spoke to this group about what I had been through, they understood exactly what I meant and could not only sympathise, but they could empathise and this was a big help for me. I had gone through the past couple of years insisting that nobody understands what it was like. Even medical staff that I saw, they could understand the symptoms but they didn't have any idea about what it was like.

Some of the techniques which I learnt from this group really helped me. One of them was Diaphragmatic Breathing. This is a breathing technique which is where, when you inhale, you breathe and expand your stomach, hold for a few seconds, then breathe out of your mouth. Doing this for ten minutes each day helped me relax, especially if I could feel myself getting stressed or worked up. It sounds simple, but something as easy as a breathing technique just opened my eyes to how I could live my life differently.

A lot of the other techniques we learnt about in the group, are ones which you would know already, such as exercise and healthy eating, but the one which really got me, was this idea of being calm and relaxed. For as long as I can remember, I have never relaxed, I have never just sat there calmly and just relaxed. I was so scared of doing it in case I would start panicking. Such an easy concept when I look back now or you as the reader thinking about it, but for me at the time, it was completely alien.

We spoke about prescription drugs and which ones we had been prescribed. The drugs I was taking made me tired in the mornings. The way I can describe the side effects of these drugs would be like waking up from a night out every morning, where your recollections of the night before are a bit foggy.

I wanted to stop taking the drugs. I wanted to manage this myself. My opinion of dealing with my anxiety and low moods is that it would be very easy to just neutralise your symptoms with strong drugs. I think that this is a good thing for people in the short term, you are kept calm and stable whilst you deal with whatever it is that is making you feel this way. But it is not a long term solution, otherwise you will become reliant on whatever it is you're taking. I cannot speak for anybody else, but what certainly helped me more than any drug, was being able to speak to like-minded people, who had suffered with the same things. But I still kept on taking them anyway, just to be sure. I did experiment on not taking them for a bit to see how I would react, because I felt OK, but after a period of about a week, I would start getting back my old symptoms. So at least I knew the drugs were working, I just needed more time before I was ready to stop taking them.

After finishing the sessions, I could slowly start seeing a light at the end of a tunnel. Something as simple as just speaking with people about what you suffer from, could help you so much. Just by talking through things and realising that you aren't alone in this and being given a podium to express your feelings, gave me hope that I would get better. I couldn't recognise myself. What I was doing now was completely different to anything I had done in the past. But it was working, I could feel it. When I came home after the sessions, I was completely exhausted, probably from opening up old wounds that I never allowed to heal.

I suppose whenever you are dealing with something challenging, you revert to type or you do something which you are comfortable with; for example, I kept myself busy. But I think what was really helping me in particular, was trying something new. I did this because what I was doing at the time wasn't working, and I was reluctant to try anything new because I was scared that I would get worse. In fact, I felt a million times better for trying something new. Whenever I think back to this now, especially when I am about to do something or try something I haven't done before, then I think, "What have I got to lose? Just go with an open mind and see what happens."

During one of their final visits to my home, the brain injury team came to deliver the results of my test. I was a little nervous as I didn't know what it would show. Even if it did, I knew in my heart that there was nothing wrong with my brain, it functioned just as well as it always did. I knew that the problems I was having were nothing to do with any long lasting brain damage. The results confirmed that my brain was completely normal and there was nothing highlighting as a problem from the tests. This confirmed what I already thought at the time and, once that had been confirmed, I knew that everything I had suffered had been solely down to some sort of post-traumatic stress which I hadn't dealt with.

Although I was happy that nothing was wrong with my brain, I knew that I had changed, and that I would have to learn to live with it. As I found the fatigue management group really beneficial to me, I wanted to be able to speak about things further on a one to one basis. I was getting into the swing of opening up and now that I was happy nothing was wrong with my brain, I needed to carry on with my recovery by trying to reduce the emotional side effects.

I told the doctors that I was thinking about having some counselling. They recommended that I saw a neuropsychologist as they would perhaps provide me with some answers.

During my sessions with the neuropsychologist, I completely opened up. I had never spoken this openly to someone before, not even during the fatigue management sessions. It was strange at first, I didn't really want to let anyone in to reveal the skeletons in my closet. For one, I was embarrassed that I thought this way and I didn't want to be judged for thinking like that. But, I had come this far and I had to see it through. I surprised myself at how open I was, how vulnerable I felt when speaking to the psychologist. I wouldn't say that I was a guarded person, but I have certainly been reluctant to tell anyone if something was wrong with me. I had a problem with showing weakness to people, unless I really felt comfortable with them.

The sessions were very helpful and therapeutic. In the fatigue management group I spoke briefly about thoughts and feelings, as well as listening to other people's experiences. This, on the other hand, was completely one on one. I spoke for about an hour about anything and everything relating to what I had been experiencing. If I stopped talking, then there would be a silence, which I then would fill by talking more and more. Towards the end, the neuropsychologist would offer her advice on what they think would be the best thing for me and how they have interpreted what I have told them. Even after being in the fatigue management group, I hadn't ever opened up this much before, but I knew I needed to let it all out and get it off my chest, otherwise I cannot get on with my life, leaving things buried.

I went into this reluctantly, with nowhere else to turn, and ended up feeling a million times better as a result. When I think about the groups, the counselling and the visits to my home, I think that the answers I needed to defeat my problems, I already had. What these different groups and meetings did, was to provide me with a platform to speak openly about them. I had been speaking to myself for over three years and I was convincing myself to keep quiet and not say anything. I was convincing myself to get quick fixes to alleviate any problems I was facing.

When I look back at the last couple of years, I am proud of what I have been able to achieve and that I have still been able to carry on with my life as normal. Every time I see old pictures of myself or reminisce about the things I have done, I always think to myself, "but behind the smile, I was screaming inside." But I have to take the positives from what I have done and not regret what I didn't get sorted at the time.

Even though it was probably the worst time of my life being in the hospital waiting for Tom to get better, it did bring out some positives. It showed me what it's like from the other side. It also brought all our family even closer together. But it also allows you to put things into perspective. I remember being back in work when Tom was home and me and my dad were in a meeting with someone and he said to them, 'After what happened to Ben, you think to yourself, there is no point in worrying about small things, they don't bear in comparison to the greater things in life such as your family. But, once Ben had got better, you slowly fall back into the same routine and start picking up the bad habits again. Then, with what happened to Tom, it's like a kick up the backside to remind you again.' I remember him saying that and thinking, yes you are right (I didn't say this to him at the time!) the little things don't matter, think about what is important.

What was important was my family, my happiness and my health. I was in a position now to draw a line under everything, not to let this define me, but to make me a better person. I started to think about ways in which I could take the positives from everything, to adopt the techniques I had learnt from speaking in the groups and also during the home visits and to start putting them into practice.

I thought of ways in which I could help myself even more, to achieve the happiness I had been craving for so long. I was tired of seeking out artificial "quick fixes" to feel happy or content, I wanted it to happen organically. Everything I had tried over the years had eventually failed. They worked for a short while, but I never dealt with what was causing my problems and they would end up rearing their head over and over again. I was tired of waiting for it to happen again.

I had everything I needed and wanted right there in front of me. A supportive family, Sian, Erin and even Dotty and I needed to start to focus on that more.

I started to feel alive again and I wanted it to continue.

14- Brain Injury Survivor's Guide to Life on Earth

I am sat here now, writing the final part of my book, Erin is crawling after Dotty, Sian is watching what they are both up to, and I am sat in the garden, looking for inspiration for this final section. What can I take from everything that has happened?

I went from not wanting to write about myself and my experiences, to actually enjoy doing it. When writing, things would crop up in my head and I would remember something that had happened. Even when I read through what I have written, it doesn't sound believable even to me, and it's so far-fetched. But it's all true and it's up to me and me alone, to use these events to my advantage.

I have been pondering over this last section for a while as this is me looking back at everything and wondering what this all means and what advice or help I can offer the reader. How do I bunch everything that had happened up into a little parcel and shelve away, whilst at the same time, taking what I need out of it? Well, through reading, researching, reflecting on the past few years and being honest with myself, I have developed techniques which have changed my life.

When I look back now at what happened over the past couple of years, although I went through some great times and had some great experiences, I wasn't truly happy. I was just kidding myself thinking that I would be able to cope with what had happened and use my coping mechanisms to deal with anything that came my way. But I was stupid to think that it would just go away. I was ignorant to how this could affect my life in a big way and how it was much bigger and much more powerful than I ever realised and a lot more than I could cope with.

The one thing I would tell anybody who has had any sort of life changing event, or are suffering from any sort of anxiety related illness, to get help. Swallow your pride, and cast aside any doubts you have in opening up to people, because it really does work. At the end of the day, the people that you are speaking to are, more often than not, paid to deal with this sort of thing and are qualified to offer you advice. I can only speak for myself, but imagine many people are reluctant to talk about their feelings. Getting help doesn't have to be any sort of counselling, it could just be something as simple as telling a loved one or a friend. Getting it off your chest and hopefully you will pick someone who can offer you their opinion, to look at things from an outsider's perspective. I look back now and I cannot believe how I was able to manage life with keeping everything bottled up. I had managed to make myself ignorant to anything that was going on and had manoeuvred through the side effects and managed to convince everyone that I was OK, to the detriment of my own health.

It helped me in so many ways, being able to speak with a third party, who knew nothing about me and could look at things from a completely different angle. They didn't know what I was like beforehand, so are just treating me as I am now. The groups that I attended for fatigue management helped me to connect with like-minded people who had been through something similar. I met a whole variety of different people, at different stages in their lives, who had all had their lives put on hold with what had happened. Although we all had different ways of interpreting what had happened, and even though all our brains were different, there was a common theme running through all of our stories, which allowed us all to empathise with each other. Like I said earlier, you feel so much lighter after speaking with people, you can get things off your chest, you don't feel guilty for burdening people with what you have to say, you don't feel like you are being judged, you don't feel like you're going mad for what you are going through.

Alongside my fatigue management group I also had some counselling sessions. This is also something which I would highly recommend. Depending on what country you are from, you can get counselling services for free. You can also find counsellors as a paid service, but it is definitely worth the money. The length of time that I wandered around in my life, keeping things bottled up inside me, not telling anybody. They would eventually leave my thought process, but would remain unresolved. Nobody knows you better than yourself, but at the same time, your definitions on things that you think about can sometimes be misconstrued and not based on anything, other than your opinion. If you think about it logically, a counsellor or a medical professional, may have seen similar symptoms to yours countless times, whereas you are only dealing with what you had experienced personally. So their advice is worth taking, it is worth asking them for help. Even if you don't really like the advice they give you, it is extremely cathartic to just vent to somebody, whilst they sit there and listen.

I know that my brain injury had changed who I was. I knew that I didn't think in the same way as I used to. I can remember who I was beforehand and who I am now. It has been a very frustrating journey to try and come to terms with the changes I have gone through, but there has to come a point where you just accept that it has happened. No amount of regret, anxiety or frustration is going to bring it back. Where possible, you can turn these changes to your advantage. I would spend forever, looking back at who I was and what I was like before my accident, but it didn't get me anywhere, it just made me feel worse.

The changes that I have encountered did put a massive strain on my relationship with Sian in particular. She had stayed with me all this time and accepted that I had changed who I was, but still loved me regardless of that. This is something which is really hard to take. At first, I was nonchalant about any changes to my personality, because I thought to myself, "well, I'm alive aren't I?" It then slowly turned into frustration because I had changed and I couldn't reverse what had happened.

Now that I can look back and reflect, I have learnt to accept what has happened. It is something very unique to brain injury survivors, in that whatever you have suffered during the injury changes how your brain works which, in turn, changes you. What I would say to this is that you must, in whatever capacity, accept it. This is difficult I know, but you will have to accept it sooner or later if you want to be happy. Try, where possible, to turn what has happened into an advantage. If it hadn't happened to me, then I wouldn't think the way I do now. There are things which never used to bother me, bother me now. There are things which get me irate, there are things which cause me to react more than they would have done. How I can turn this into an advantage for myself, I am not so sure.

I have learnt to accept what has happened and have tried to embrace the changes to my personality, however difficult they might be. To sit and watch whilst my family put up with my changes is my inspiration. Their unconditional love during what must have been a very difficult time was unbelievable. If they can learn to live with it and still love me the same then surely I can accept it as well. They loved the "new me" just as much as the "old me" and they did that without even thinking about it.

Accepting it can work both ways. You can either accept it or decide that it won't let it define your life. Or you can accept it, but remain bitter and angry about what has happened. My opinion is that it's pointless to be angry or bitter, because what will that achieve? It can't bring you back to how you were and how you used to be. Accepting it is the hardest thing to do, because, one minute you are happily living your life with your future to look forward to, and the next, your life just changes within the space of just a couple of weeks. You are being told by countless people that what has happened to you means that you can't do this or you can't do that. You notice that you don't behave the same way, you don't think the same way, and you don't feel the same person. That is a lot to take for anybody and it's extremely hard to accept. Even somebody from the outside looking in, you can sympathise with the person as it changes their lives forever almost immediately, but for you to go through it yourself, it's completely different. If you have had something life changing happen to you and you are reading this now, then all I would say is that you will get through it. Please learn to accept it. I know it's hard, but your life will be better for it. Your life would never have been how you envisaged it and this is just a meander on your life's journey. Take advantage of it. You can now do things or have an outlook on things that you would never have had. Your experiences of what you have gone through sets you aside from so many people.

I suppose for a lot of people with similar side effects to what I have had this is the problem, you have to be honest with yourself and admit there is something wrong. Even as recent as one year ago I wouldn't have even considered going to speak to somebody or go to a group, but it has made me more aware and a better person. The "keeping busy" mantra which I have followed is great if you have things to keep you busy, but it doesn't make you happy and it certainly doesn't get rid of the symptoms in the long term. A lot of people turn to quick fixes when they have these symptoms as they want a short term fix. Again, great for ten minutes, but in the long run you end up worse as a result. I was denying what had happened. I knew that I had been hijacked to some degree by new personality traits and behaviours which were unwelcome in my life, but I tried to avoid their existence and just convinced myself that I had always been this way.

Having a brain injury changes who you are, both physically and mentally. I think that living with a brain injury is something which is quite unique. You need to accept that it has happened, and accept the limitations you now have. But with it, comes new possibilities, you have come through a life threatening situation and survived. What you have gone through, what you have suffered both physically and mentally, you should use to your advantage. When I look at it now, I had a choice, I could either be bitter the rest of my life and regret what had happened, or I could just accept what had happened. I chose the latter, because being bitter and regretting it wouldn't get me anywhere, and I would constantly live in the past.

Something else which I have found has helped me enormously has been to change my reading habits. I have always been quite an avid reader, but I had mainly stuck to reading history books, both fiction and non-fiction. Whilst I enjoy them and find them all fascinating, I thought that it might help to read different types of books and be more open to them. Reading is a great way of taking yourself out of a situation, just by putting your mind somewhere else during the period you are reading.

I had started to read books which talk about how your brain works. Through understanding my brain in more detail, I became familiar with why certain things happen and why I behave in certain ways at different times. I started to read books about people who have had similar accidents to mine, to better appreciate how it affects different people and how they dealt with it. I also read about real life experiences of people, such as traumatic events they went through and how they dealt with them.

Something as simple as changing my reading habits benefited me so much. When reading, my mind wanders as it always does, but this time, I was wandering into the writer's life and understanding things from their perspective.

I can now, to some degree, understand and appreciate my anxiety and panicking. I already know when my low moods are coming. When they are coming, it's like the Simon and Garfunkel song, 'Sound Of Silence', and the lyric, 'hello darkness my old friend'. In the past, I have become low, being caught out by it and not being able to put something in the way of it to take my mind off it. The thoughts you have during these low periods are not logical, they are far-fetched, extreme and often not true. It made me reckless. Reckless with my health, my state of mind and with my relationships with my family and friends. I would always get them at the weekend, and sometimes during the end of the week. Now I don't get them as often, they come and go with the passing of time. Just because I am able to limit the effects they have and the frequency of them, I still have bad days. You will always have bad days, it's about accepting that you have them and remember that they will pass with time and the happiness will return. I am not a robot and I am controlled by my emotions some of the time, so this will inevitably happen.

I tackled my anxiety by starting to anticipate my weekend blues, as well as any other times during the week when I would feel this way. I started keeping a journal of only what I was getting anxious over. As an example, I would worry about something in work, I would explore different scenarios, and end up in a blind panic over it. Now, after writing them all down, I dissect each of them when I am in a good place, trying to understand whether any of these thoughts have any basis. They don't. I only look and go through my journal once I was feeling OK. I would read through what I was worrying over. In some cases, what I was worrying over had already passed, and wasn't nearly as bad as I thought it would be. I have been doing this for a few months and it really works. When you are in that state, nobody can tell you any different, they are legitimate concerns and worries and there is no way that you can be told otherwise. However, once you've calmed and you are in a good place, reading back through them, dissecting what you were thinking, you can understand them better.

The way I look at it, your brain is developing these anxious thoughts, and you need to deal with them, not ignore them or try and avoid them. By dealing with them, you are training your brain in a way to not react as much next time. So, for example, if you were worrying about what somebody thought of you, you wrote this down, then, after a period once you had calmed, you revisited the same thought, you could answer the anxiety. So you could think to yourself, why am I concerned what this person thinks of me? Well, they are my boss, so I am concerned what they think. But then you could say, well I have worked as hard as I could, I have been honest and conscientious. If the boss still does not think well of me, then there is nothing more that I can do. Next time this thought crops up in your head during a period of anxiety, you have already dealt with this earlier and it should hopefully prevent you getting anxious or panicky over it. It is a way of training your brain to come up with logical ways of answering your anxiety, in a constructive and healthy way.

Along with the changes I have made in my life, I had made sure that I only surround myself by people who benefit me, as well as me benefiting them, like a sort of mutually beneficial relationship. I have tried my best to reduce the time I spend with people who do not benefit my life at all, if anything, they make it worse. We all know people who suck the life from you, who like to moan constantly at you and drain all your energy. We all know people who try and put you down and try and belittle you. Well, where possible, and if it bothers you, try and avoid the time you spend with them, it will only make you feel worse. Whether this is through not socialising with them, or even changing your job, the more you spend time with these people, the worse you will end up feeling if you are the type of person to be affected by it. Everybody, including myself, like to have a good moan now and again, but you will understand exactly what I mean when you think of people in your life who fit the criteria I set out before.

I try, where possible, to give myself periods during the week where I can just be at peace, with no distractions. This can be anything from being in your bedroom, or living room, in the peace and quiet, or with some music on, where you can just be, without any distractions. One of the ways I achieve this is through doing yoga. I know this is not for everyone, but it really helps me relax, especially during periods of high anxiety. I never thought yoga would be for me, I just didn't associate with it at all. When my anxiety is at its worse, I feel as though somebody is screaming in my head and I just want to scream, "Shut up!" Doing yoga helps me channel these types of things out, I am just focusing on keeping the positions during the hour, focusing on my breathing and just being sat, totally relaxed. I come out refreshed and a lot calmer than I was an hour before. If I can't do yoga, then I will spend time in my room, just sat, quietly, listening to music. This type of relaxation was difficult for me as I suffered from anxiety, as the peace and quiet and nothing to think about was a dangerous recipe. I was only able to relax and be at peace once I started to address what was making me anxious. But then I suppose everybody is different and perhaps spending time in the quiet and relaxing might reduce your anxiety.

One of the final things I had done which has probably helped me the most, is by having commandments to live by. If you have a faith, then you already have commandments to live by. In fact, most people in the world live by obeying commandments. Most of us wouldn't steal, wouldn't kill somebody, wouldn't cheat and wouldn't do many of the things which most legal systems class as illegal. But what I mean by commandments is having a set of personal rules which you live by. These are the things which make you happy, the things which matter. Anything which is not on this list of commandments, does not matter as much.

My commandments are quite simple. To be happy, to put Erin and Sian first, to be healthy, to feel fulfilled. Any situation I am presented with in my life, any decisions that I need to make, I always refer to these commandments. If they don't meet the criteria, then I won't do it. It's pretty simple in theory, but it takes a bit of time to get your head around it. When you stick to these rules then, eventually, it becomes a lot easier to make decisions.

For example, should I move jobs? Well, will it make me happy? Yes, because I am currently not happy in my current job. Am I putting Erin and Sian first? Yes, because if I am happier, then we have a better home life. Will it make me healthier? Yes, because I will be less stressed. Will I feel fulfilled? This is a difficult one because you are changing jobs and can only guess based on the limited information that you have on whether you will feel fulfilled. But on the balance of the answers to the previous questions, then the answer is quite simple. I find that if I do things which are against what my beliefs or rules are, then eventually, I will become unhappy. Life is all about having a balance, not doing too many of one thing or too little of another. Stick to your morals or your commandments and you will find the balance in your life.

Think of this quote from the great Albert Einstein, "Insanity: doing the same thing over and over again and expecting different results."

If you are unhappy with something and don't do anything about it, then it will never change. Just be honest with yourself and make the changes you need. If you sit back and look at what is making you unhappy, you will probably find that you are going against what you believe in. Make the necessary changes that are in line with what you believe in and it should sort itself out.

Everybody's idea of happiness is completely unique, but regardless of this the effects will be the same. If you aren't true to yourself then it will eventually come back to bite you.

When I think about the pain of the accident, by pain I mean physical pain, I didn't feel any because I don't remember. I was definitely awake as that's what I was told, I jumped up after being knocked down. I would imagine that, at that time, I would have been in quite considerable pain, yet I don't remember anything. I have wondered why that is, and, for want of a better answer, my opinion is that my subconscious kicked in and shielded my conscious self away from the pain. It blocked it out so I wouldn't experience it. It's a strange feeling when you think of it that way. So many times now I am in a situation where I think to myself, I am conscious, aware of everything that's going on, so something bad isn't imminent. I know that's not a great way to think all the time but what I mean by this is I don't worry anymore. I don't worry about death, I don't worry about something bad happening, because if it did, I wouldn't know anything about it.

How many times have you heard the phrases, "treat each day as if it's your last," or, "live in the moment." How many of you do it? I certainly didn't. If anything, I would scoff at people who said that, as I thought they were just reckless people not planning for the future. If I was being honest with myself, I don't think I really understood what it meant, and because I didn't understand it, I just laughed it off.

But, after what has happened to me, and also Tom, I get it now. My interpretation of it is not literally treating each day as if it's your last, but not holding back on things. Obviously, planning for the future is a good thing and it's very wise to make sure that you have a plan for your future. But there is a difference in doing this, and preventing yourself from doing things because of some distance milestone you need to reach. Saying things to yourself such as, I'll go on holiday once the house is done. Or, I want to change career but I am scared of it not working. Or even, I should really ring my friend and see how they are, or, I really should keep in touch with that family member. All of these things are put off by millions of people every day. I cannot comment on this for certain, but I would be confident that, as you look at an older version of yourself, coming towards the end of your life, when you think of these things, and in particular the ones you didn't do, would you regret it? Did those things that you worried about so much when you were younger turn out all that bad?

To put it into perspective, whilst I was writing this book, I had been thinking to myself recently that I needed to speak to Tom more about his head injury and see if I could help at all. If you remember earlier I had taken a step back so as not to affect him at all in his recovery, but I did think that I could at least offer him something. But, I did what many people do and put it off, I thought, "I'll do it tomorrow." I was also not sure how to approach him and talk to him about it.

One afternoon, I was out with Sian, Erin and her parents having lunch, when I got a phone call from my dad. I answered it in a frustrated tone because I wanted to eat my dinner! "Hello, you OK?" "Yes son. I am just ringing to let you know that Tom has had quite a bad seizure when he was in the car with Paul." Paul was a colleague from work. "Is he OK?" I said. "I think so," Dad said, "but he doesn't know where he is and he's bleeding and has been sick." I know nothing should ever surprise me, especially in my life, but it always catches you off guard. I just felt sick. "I'll meet you at the hospital," I said to Dad.

When I got to the hospital, Tom was looking OK, but quite confused. He did gradually get better during the hours in hospital. He had a number of tests to ascertain what had happened. The doctors said that anybody with a brain injury is at risk with seizure, but it can increase the chances quite a bit if they are doing too much. Tom was currently working full time, as well as renovating a house he had bought to rent out. He had been doing too much and his brain just couldn't take it, I suppose.

Thinking about it when I left the hospital after he had been discharged, I immediately thought to myself, "if only I'd phoned him when I said, maybe this wouldn't have happened." I had procrastinated over and over again. But, as my dad said, life has a way of giving you "gentle" reminders now and again. These "gentle" reminders not only let you put things into perspective, but it also gives you the kick to do things you put off.

So, at the crux of it all, I am here today, alive and well, my brother, alive and well, and I am thinking to myself, "What do I take from all this?" I am in a very unique position, not only have I been at death's door and taken almost four years to recover from it, but I am seeing it happening to my brother unfold before my eyes. The first thing I will do is make sure that my brother has the help that I never got. Tom is currently under the care of the acute brain injury service. He will get the support he needs and address anything before it grows. Me and Tom are completely different people. Tom thinks differently to me. I would sit and worry about something over and over again until I was in a state of panic, whereas Tom, although he might have this in him, he has a different outlook on life.

I have been lucky in a way. Although I have been in a bad way, there are many other people that are a lot worse off than I am, and I am just thankful that I am able to write this book, live my life relatively normal and do the things I want to do. There are so many people in the world worse off, and they are so brave to continue through life without complaining or being bitter about what's happened. Sometimes I feel a bit of a fraud moaning about things that have happened to me when there are other people in a much worse situation. My best friend Mia, who, after what happened to her, has carried on with her life regardless and she is an inspiration to not only me, but everyone who knows her. She could have easily remained bitter and angry about what had happened to her, but instead, has grabbed life with two hands and done things which even I wouldn't do. I have been with her when she has been bungee jumping, flying in a helicopter, in-door sky diving and travelled to places such as Gambia, Florida and Morocco.

I have literally been through hell the past couple of years despite having some wonderful moments to cherish. If I had been in a better place, then I would have appreciated the moments more, rather than now looking back. I wish I would have lived in the moment more and just enjoyed what I was doing right at that time, rather than kicking myself over the past and thinking too much into the future.

The injuries to both me and Tom have created limitations on our lives and we need to both accept what has happened. But with these limitations come new possibilities and challenges which we need to find and embrace them. Both our lives have forked off course, and it's up to us to go with the new route and live life under these new conditions. We cannot reverse what has happened and get back onto the old route, which has now gone.

I sincerely hope that you, the reader, can take something from this book. I hope that my experiences and how I dealt with them in two different ways gives you some food for thought in your life. It took me to nearly lose my brother to realise what was important and what I had been doing wrong all this time. I implore that you try and find that thing that makes you happy, that you live by what you stand for and you live completely in the moment.

I wish all my readers a happy and rewarding life.

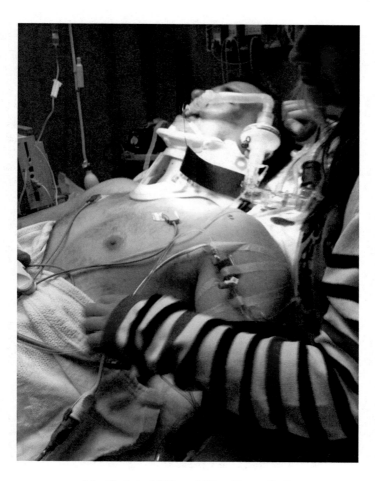

Me, Sedated When I Was Brought In

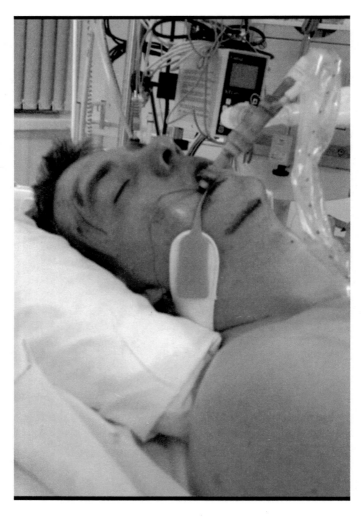

Me in a Coma

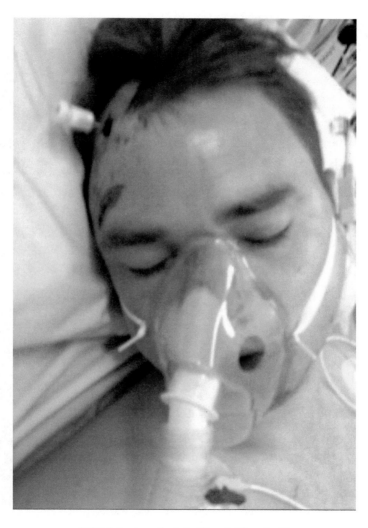

ICP Monitor in My Head (Top Left)

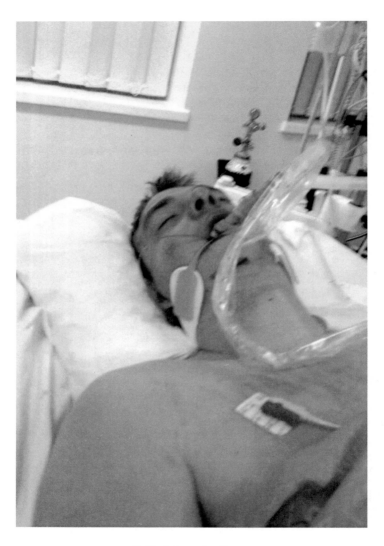

Still Asleep in Coma

Me, resting after Coming Home

The Day I Got Dotty

Egypt 2012

Marriage

Hawaii Honeymoon

Run or Dye Charity Event with Mia

Me and My Friend Mia on a Helicopter Ride

Sian Pregnant

Arrival of Erin

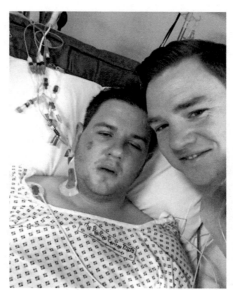

Tom Waking Up

Tom More or Less Fully Awake

Erin and Dotty